FOUNDATIONS OF DISTANCE EDUCATION
Second Edition

DESMOND KEEGAN

Routledge
London and New York

First published 1986 by Croom Helm
Second edition by Routledge 1990
11 New Fetter Lane, London EC4P 4EE

Simultaneously published in the USA and Canada
by Routledge
a division of Routledge, Chapman and Hall, Inc.
29 West 35th Street, New York, NY 10001

© 1986, 1990 Desmond Keegan

Printed and bound in Great Britain by
Biddles Ltd, Guildford and King's Lynn

British Library Cataloguing in Publication Data

Keegan, Desmond
    Foundations of distance education. - 2nd ed.
    1. Distance study
    I. Title
    371.3

    ISBN 0-415-03162-1
         0-415-01052-7

Library of Congress Cataloging in Publication Data

Keegan, Desmond.
        Foundations of distance education / Desmond Keegan. - 2nd ed.
        p. cm.
        Includes index.
        ISBN 0-415-03162-1. - ISBN 0-415-01052-7 (pbk.)
        1. Distance education. I. Title.
    LC5800.K43   1990
    378′.03–dc20   89-10318
                                                          CIP

Foundations of distance education

Second edition

For
Patricia
and
Martin

CONTENTS

FIGURES

TABLES

PREFACE

It came as a pleasant surprise to learn from Routledge early in 1988 that *Distance Education: International Perspectives*, the reader I published with Börje Holmberg and David Sewart in 1984, was to be reprinted in paperback. Later in 1988 came the request to prepare a second education of *Foundations of Distance Education*. It was to be a somewhat slimmer volume than the first edition to facilitate publication in paperback as well as hard cover.

The second edition has given me the opportunity to correct errors in the first edition and make use of recently published work. I have chosen to prune the sections on distance education in practice from the first edition rather than the theoretical sections.

Distance education is an international phenomenon and I have tried to present this dimension in both the first and second editions of this book. The student will get valuable insights into this form of education from the east and the west, from countries with advanced technological systems and from others with less developed economies.

The major focus of the 1970s was the foundation of the open universities; the impressive systems being developed in Asia are a new centre of interest for the 1990s.

Desmond Keegan,
Adelaide

Part I

THE CONCEPT OF DISTANCE EDUCATION

Chapter One

THE STUDY OF DISTANCE EDUCATION

It is the development of distance education as an academic discipline that will have the most profound effect on its practice in the future.

Eric Gough, 1984

CONTEXT

In the 1980s distance education emerged as a standard component of the provision of education in many national systems. In contrast with conventional education which is oral and group-based, distance education shatters the interpersonal communication of face-to-face provision and disperses the learning group throughout the nation.

By harnessing industrialized processes to education and responding to the growth of privacy and loss of the sense of community which are characteristics of post-industrial society, distance education has opened access to study towards all levels of qualification to the working adult - the student who continues to contribute to the nation's Gross National Product throughout the length of his or her study programme.

In 1983 Sewart of the Open University (UK) wrote:

The last decade has seen a phenomenal growth in distance education and the integration of this method of education into the standard educational provision in a large number of countries to such an extent that it is now no longer possible to think solely in the traditional sense of face-to-face contact.

(Sewart 1983:5)

For long the Cinderella of the education spectrum, distance education emerged in the 1970s with a changed image. It has

3

recently come of age after a chequered and often criticized first hundred years.

Furthermore, its future seems assured because of the growing privatization of life in many developed western societies and the incapacity of on-campus programmes to cope with even minimal educational opportunity elsewhere.

The improvement of distance education in the 1970s was both qualitative and quantitative. It can be attributed to:

• the development of new communications technology (Bates 1982; Ruggles *et al.* 1982);
• a growing sophistication in the use of printed materials (Daniel and Stroud 1981);
• improved design of instructional materials (Holmberg 1981);
• improved provision of support services for students studying at a distance (Sewart 1978); and
• the foundation in 1969 of the Open University (UK) at Milton Keynes and the subsequent foundation of a series of similar structures in both developed and developing countries (Rumble and Keegan 1982).

Despite the euphoria of claims like Sewart's it is clear that distance education is little known and little studied. Even a cursory reading of educational literature shows that distance systems are usually ignored. They merit not a paragraph in most volumes of educational philosophy, in guides to administrative practice or in analyses of didactic strategy.

When it is not ignored, it can be seen - in the harsher funding atmosphere of the 1980s - as an unwanted competitor. The time has come for taking stock. Not all the portents are favourable. Writing in 1984, the Australian distance educator, Gough, proposed that 'it is the development of distance education as an academic discipline that will have the most profound effect on its practice in the future' (1984:25).

This book is an attempt to contribute to such a development.

AIMS

This book attempts to respond to the call made over a decade ago by Moore, then of the University of Wisconsin at Madison and today at Pennsylvania State University:

As we continue to develop various non-traditional methods

of reaching the growing numbers of people who cannot, or who will not, attend conventional institutions but who choose to learn apart from their teachers, we should direct some of our resources to the macrofactors:

- describing and defining the field
- discriminating between the various components of this field
- identifying the critical elements of the various forms of teaching and learning
- building a theoretical framework which will embrace this whole area of education.

(Moore 1973:661)

Moore's call went largely unheeded. A theoretical framework to embrace this whole area of education has yet to be erected. This is grave because distance education purports to make available a parallel provision of education to that of conventional schools, colleges, and universities. Unlike other methods of teaching or modes of operation with which they are sometimes bracketed, distance systems claim to provide a complete educational coverage, equal in quality and status to that of conventional provision, encompassing every stage of the educational process from application, enrolment, and counselling through to examination and certification many years later.

Most research in this field has been practical rather than theoretical. While research on the practice of distance education is important and fundamental it is incidental and peripheral to a firmly based theory of distance education. A theory is something that eventually can be reduced to a phrase, a sentence or a paragraph and which, while subsuming all the practical research, gives the foundation on which structures of need, purpose, and administration can be erected. A firmly based theory of distance education will be one which can provide the touchstone against which decisions - political, financial, educational, and social - can be taken with confidence. Such a theoretical basis would replace the *ad hoc* way of responding to 'crisis' situations which normally characterize this field of education.

PREMISES

In attempting to provide a guide to theory and practice in distance education the following assumptions are made:

- Distance education is a coherent and distinct field of educational endeavour: it embraces programmes at a distance at primary and secondary, technical and further, college and university levels in both public and private sectors. It has existed for somewhat over 100 years and is to be found today in most countries.
- Distance education is a system of education. It can provide a complete educational programme for both children and adults outside of, and distinct from, conventional, oral, group-based provision. It has its own laws of didactical structure and its own quasi-industrial administrative procedures.
- Distance education is a form of education fraught with problems for administrators, teachers, and students. It is characterized by the fragility of the non-traditional in education. These difficulties concern the quantity, quality, and status of education at a distance. Good practice in distance education seeks to provide solutions for these inherent difficulties.
- Distance education is a needed component of most national educational systems.

This study does not seek to promote distance education. Rather it seeks to analyse it from as neutral a standpoint as possible and present it with both its strengths and weaknesses underlined. In doing this an attempt is made not to limit the research to the English-speaking tradition in education because the contribution of the English-speaking countries is only a part of a much more complex whole. Thus much of the basic distance education research in the period 1960-70 was done in German; the basic institutional model is probably French; in recent years much progress has been reported from Spanish-speaking countries; and this book is a much altered version of a series of lectures first delivered in Italian.

THE STUDY OF EDUCATION

Where does the study of distance education lie within the discipline of education? Many universities have a faculty for teaching and research in the discipline of education. Most faculties of education are subdivided into departments or fields of teaching and research. Most faculties of education carry on research and teach in a selection of fields depending on student need, staff expertise, or government direction. Some of the fields (philosophy of education, educational psychology) are often regarded as essential. Some (special education) are in vogue today; some (comparative education) are in decline. Some (adult education, distance education, educational administration, educational technology) are more specialized and departments dealing with these fields may not be found in many universities.

This book regards distance education as a distinct field of educational research and teaching within the discipline of education. It is considered to have links to other fields within the discipline of education, notably educational technology, adult education, and the study of non-traditional/open systems.

HISTORY OF DISTANCE EDUCATION RESEARCH

Academic research in distance education reached a level of maturity compatible with the emergence of a new field within education by the early 1970s. Although noteworthy contributions had been made by individual researchers, amongst whom one would certainly include Childs (1963, 1988) from the University of Lincoln at Nebraska, Wedemeyer (1981) from the University of Wisconsin at Madison and Holmberg (1960) from Malmö in Sweden, the major development came from a group of researchers whom I propose to call 'The Tübingen Group'.

The Tübingen Group comprised, amongst others, Dohmen (1967), Graff (1964), Peters (1965), Rebel (1971), and Delling (1966). To this group can be attributed the identification of what Sparkes (1983) calls 'the emergence of a new set of problems which is essential for an academic discipline'. By the early 1970s the Tübingen Group had published at least sixty research studies in a number of series of which the most important were *Tübinger Beiträger zum Fernstudium* and *Studien und Berichte zum Fernstudium im Medienverbund*. Dohmen and Peters, in particular, had defined and established the extent of the field, Delling had determined its history, and Peters had identified its particular focus which distinguished it from all other fields of educational research.

The work of O. Peters

Outstanding among the contributions of the Tübingen Group is the work of O. Peters. Four of his studies, which are fundamental to the history of distance education research, are summarized briefly here.

1. *Der Fernunterricht. Materialien zur Diskussion einer neuen Unterrichtsform* (*Distance education. Sources for the analysis of a New Form of Teaching*) was published in 1965. In it Peters established that distance education had been in existence for 100 years and was to be found in most countries in the late 1950s. The breadth and depth of the research is impressive with detailed treatment of countries like Vietnam and Czechoslovakia that have scarcely been mentioned in the research of the last 20 years.
2. In 1968 Peters published the 550 page volume *Das Hochschulfernstudium. Materialien zur Diskussion einer neuen Studienform* on distance education at university level. He shows, among other analyses, that open universities had been in existence for 40 years.
3. *Texte zum Hochschulfernstudium* (1971) is basically a typology with contributions from Möhle, Holmberg, Childs, Wedemeyer, and others. The book has a hidden thesis that distance education has higher status in socialist education systems than capitalist ones.
4. The fundamental theoretical study of distance education, Peters' *Die didaktische Struktur des Fernunterrichts* was published in 1973. Peters proposes that the central theme of the academic study of distance education is the abandonment in that form of education of interpersonal, face-to-face communication, which was previously thought to be a cultural imperative for all education both in east and west, and its replacement by an apersonal, mechanical, or electronic 'communication' created by the technology of industrialization (see Chapter 5).

The mid-1970s to today

The Tübingen Group dispersed in the mid-1970s. Dohmen returned to the University of Tübingen, Peters and Graff transferred to the Fernuniversität, Delling and Rebel remained at the German Institute for Distance Education (DIFF). Few researchers in the English-speaking world built on the foundations laid by the Tübingen Group, though their work is cited by Holmberg, Bååth, and Wedemeyer.

The early 1970s saw the creation of a series of distance institutions for whom 'newness' was politically important. These institutions seemed slow to align themselves with an established field, in existence for 100 years, found in every country of the world, which said that open universities had been in existence since the 1920s and for which the central focus was the abandonment of what had been a cultural imperative for university education since its inception. Researchers tended to align themselves with established fields of research that had a similarity to distance education but which would vigorously defend the role of interpersonal communication in education (adult education, educational technology). By the late 1970s terminology was clarified and progress was made towards definition (see Chapter 3).

The 1980s saw an exponential growth in the literature on distance education, the foundation of a number of academic journals, and the development of research in sub-fields like course design, economics of distance education, student support services, and media in distance education. With the mid-1980s came the first courses for university credit in distance education from the Fernuniversität, South Australian College of Advanced Education, Deakin University, Pennsylvania State University, and the Association of European Correspondence Schools.

METHODOLOGY

Considerable thought in preparing this study has been given to evolving a methodology for presenting the reader with a guide to this field of educational activity. A methodology was needed that would lead to knowledge and understanding. It had to be capable of describing and defining the field of distance education; it had to discriminate between the institutional types, the didactic strategies, the varying media that constitute this field; it had to be able to identify both those forms of teaching and learning which are seen as constituents of distance education and those that lie outside it.

In order to be successful as a guide, the methodology chosen had to be able to take account of the context and complexity of the field and to get to the real phenomenon of distance education and not some 'scientific' abstraction. It had to cover 100 years of history and the worldwide activity of the present time.

As well as charting the fragile theoretical underpinnings that scholars have supplied to date, the aim was to provide a guide to help administrators make sensible decisions and to help practitioners choose good models. Scientific research is ill at ease in the context of a guide. The controlled experiment, which is the lynch-pin of science's insistence on the reproducibility of data, involves ensuring that the normal variability of the environment is kept within specified limits. It is exactly the variability of the environment that a good guide should reflect. Further, the nature of scientific research, in which one attempts to analyse educational problems in terms of distinct causal theories, is out of place in an area where management rather than pedagogy is the key problem encountered. When the management of quasi-industrial processes is central to an educational system what is needed is not normative scientific study of special approaches to pedagogy but problem-based case studies that can provide guides to good practice. Happily, narrow scientific research is not the only way to knowledge and understanding. Other methods can lead to valid explanations of the complex world of distance education systems.

PROCEDURE

The methodology adopted attempts to be synergistic, that is, it attempts to find a way to cope with the complexity of the educational environment and the inter-connectedness of human and institutional relationships. Another element that synergistic theories and methodologies seek to encapsulate is experience. Experience is of particular importance in this study: we are concerned here with the experience of the dedicated distance education tutor, the experience and common sense of the practised administrator, and it is important that such experience should not be eliminated by the methodology chosen.

In its actual execution, the study developed in four stages with extensive feedback mechanisms linking the various periods of research.

Stage 1

A Delphi-like approach was first used for a review of the literature. In the first instance this was to classify the varied terminology used at that time in the field, and then to see whether any cohesion could be found in the multiplicity of educational phenomena encountered. The bulk of the literature analysed was in English, but the considerable literature in German both from the Federal Republic of Germany and the German Democratic Republic was not ignored. Efforts were made to gather literature in French and Spanish as well, although the results were relatively meagre.

Stage 2

Distance education, however, does not exist in a vacuum: it has been in action for over 100 years. It was imperative, therefore, to see and participate in the institutions concerned.

In the period 1978-79 visits were carried out to sixty-two institutions that had been encountered in the literature. Included were structures large and small, public and private in Australia, India, United Kingdom, Netherlands, Italy, Ireland, France, German Democratic Republic, Hungary, Federal Republic of Germany, Canada and the United States of America.

The institutions ranged from correspondence schools at primary and secondary levels to open universities. Some were eliminated from the study at a later date as being general non-traditional programmes rather than a part of distance education as it came to be defined.

The institutional visits were at first structured around a framework for the analysis of distance education institutions developed by Kaye and Rumble (1981:293) at the Open University (UK). This proved too complex in practice, and was replaced by a formula developed specially for the study (see Chapter 11).

Stage 3

Initial hypotheses about the nature and structure of the groupings of educational phenomena encountered in the literature were constantly refined by feedback from the institutional case studies. This led to a period of synthesis in which patterns and hypotheses were developed for the field as a whole.

Considerable care had to be exercised at this stage because of anomalies which had been discerned between the literature search and the institutional case studies. With reference to the choice of non-print media, especially broadcast television, it quickly became evident that a disturbing amount of published research was exaggerated or inaccurate and that some of the researchers appeared not to have visited the institutions, nor even the countries, on which they were reporting.

As a result of this analysis an attempt was made to clarify

the conceptual structure and terminology of the field in an article 'On defining distance education'. A first sketch of the field as a whole was published in Germany under the title *On the Nature of Distance Education*. This provoked further feedback both in published work and in private communications.

Stage 4

As a final stage more extensive visits of up to three months in length were undertaken to a number of the institutions in Europe and North America which had emerged as central to the concept of a discipline of distance education.

INITIAL FINDINGS

As the work progressed it became clear that systemic similarities of a marked kind were present in all the institutions that fell within the definition of distance education being formulated. These similarities were the more remarkable as they cut sharply across the sectoral boundaries within which education is normally administered. They were characteristic of government primary and secondary correspondence schools, of private foundations (whether non-profit or profit-oriented), of government distance technical or further education colleges, and of open universities. Among these characteristics were:

- the absence of classrooms, lecture rooms, seminar rooms, and tutorial rooms;
- the presence of, or access to, comprehensive printing and materials production facilities;
- the absence of a library, or of places for student study, if there was a library;
- the central location of the warehouse;
- the absence of cafeterias, playgrounds, recreation facilities, drama and music amenities;
- the use of buildings which often resembled industrial offices, warehouses, or factories; and
- the fact that many of the institutions acted as post offices.

A more comprehensive listing of the characteristics of distance systems has recently been published by Rumble (1986) as pages 224-6 of his *The Planning and Management of Distance*

Education.

These divergences marked the institutions off from institutions structured for conventional, oral, group-based education in a striking and decisive way. In the case of a distance education department of an existing college or university, many of the characteristics noted were present, other things being equal, in the distance wing of the conventional institution. Here was a largely unstudied grouping of educational institutions, globally represented and growing in influence annually.

ANALYTICAL MODEL

The study had not been in progress long before it became clear that as a theoretical focus for the whole area of education being investigated, the 1973 thesis by Peters (pronounced Payters) *Die didaktische Struktur des Fernunterrichts. Untersuchungen zu einer industrialisierten Form des Lehrens und Lernens (The Didactical Structure of Distance Teaching. Investigations into an Industrial Form of Teaching and Learning)* was by far the most satisfactory explanation yet formulated. Peters' comparative research on distance institutions of all types throughout the 1960s led to his characterization of distance education as 'the most industrialised form of education'.

The conclusions of his study surprised many researchers who recoiled from the implications of the position that his comparative and theoretical analysis led him to enunciate:

> Anyone professionally involved in education is compelled to presume the existence of *two* forms of instruction which are strictly separable: traditional face-to-face teaching based on interpersonal communication *and* industrialised teaching which is based on an objectivised, rationalised, technologically-based interaction.
>
> (Peters 1973:313)

Peters had previously (1971a) complained that the normal procedures of educational research had proved of little avail in the investigations of correspondence education:

> Correspondence instruction is the most industrialised form of instruction and the usual theoretical criteria for the description of traditional instruction do not help very much in analysing correspondence instruction. (This) has

13

suggested the introduction of new categories taken from those sciences investigating the industrial production process.

(1971a:225)

Peters' rejection of the methodology of educational research as valid for an investigation of education at a distance is in contrast to those who complain that educational research methods are not adequately used in distance education.

FEEDBACK MODEL

It might be appropriate, therefore, to investigate the phenomenon of distance education by a methodology more widely used in industrial situations. Such a methodology is available in control theory, which presents a coherent set of strategies for arriving at a prescribed goal.

Control theory is normally applied to systems that are a good deal simpler than educational research systems (Sparkes 1980), nevertheless it has valuable insights to offer. Control theory deals with what are called open-loop systems and closed-loop systems.

Figure 1.1 Educational research as an open loop system

Source: Adapted from Belove and Drossman (1976)

An open-loop system (Figure 1.1) differs from a closed-loop system in that it does not contain a feedback path from output to input. The goal, namely knowledge from educational research, is obtained as far as practicable by ensuring that the inputs are correct and the system is well designed. An open-loop system is appropriate where facts rather than ideas or concepts are being researched because a good deal of knowledge can be attained by uncomplicated research. Nevertheless, as a research paradigm for distance education a closed-loop system with negative feedback is recommended.

EDUCATIONAL RESEARCH AS A CLOSED-LOOP SYSTEM WITH NEGATIVE FEEDBACK

A key concept in control theory is negative feedback. Most human activity is controlled by negative feedback loops (Sparkes 1980:12). When one writes, speaks, walks, or plays football, one watches or listens to what is happening and uses this information to control what one does. Used as a paradigm for educational research, feedback theory draws attention to the benefits to be had when errors and inadequacies are pointed out and dealt with in a way that is likely to lead to their correction.

Negative feedback processes in educational research exemplify the conversational theory of human learning in that they underline that knowledge from research is achieved by a continuous iteration of the process of absorbing new information, trying to use it and then checking whether it was correctly used. In a feedback model concepts are recycled through the research process and gradually acquire sufficient richness of meaning for them to be used with confidence to express the researcher's findings.

Figure 1.2 Educational research as a closed-loop system with negative feedback

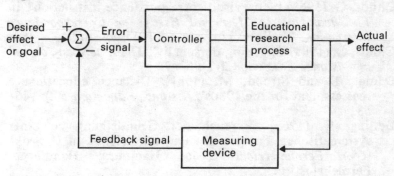

Source: Adapted from Belove and Drossman (1976)

Figure 1.2 illustrates a simple closed-loop system with negative feedback. This is a control system and the process is the educational research activity. The system input sets the goal which is the desired effect from the research. Crucial to such systems is the measurement or assessment of performance. The overall performance of the system is dominated by the effectiveness of the feedback path. By applying negative feedback in different ways it is possible to remove discrepancies and so enable the researcher to achieve the goal with greater accuracy.

In practical systems feedback paths and controllers are normally non-human and work automatically, whereas in educational research the controller is a human researcher. Thus, such models are essentially paradigms, that is, aids to the understanding of complex behaviour patterns.

Control theory provides a satisfactory methodology for the study of the phenomenon of distance education. It is synergistic, does not destroy the complexity of reality, and can encapsulate experience and common sense. Such a method can help in finding patterns in the complex reality of the world of distance systems and can provide guides for analysis.

REFERENCES

Bates, A.W. (1982) 'Trends in the use of audio-visual media in distance education systems', in Daniel *et al.* (eds) *Learning at a Distance. A World Perspective*, Edmonton: Athabasca University ICCE.

Belove, C. and Drossman, M. (1976) *Systems and Circuits for Electrical Engineering Technology*, New York: McGraw-Hill.

Childs, G. (1963) 'Supervised correspondence instruction', in *The Brandenburg Memorial Essays on Correspondence Instruction*, Madison: University of Wisconsin.

Childs, G. (1988) 'Speaking personally', *The American Journal of Distance Education* 2(2): 68–74.

Daniel, J. and Stroud, M. (1981) 'Distance education: a reassessment for the 1980s', *Distance Education* 2(2): 146–63.

Delling, R. (1966) 'Versuch der Grundelgung zu einer systematischen Theorie des Fernunterrichts, in L. Sroka (ed.) *Fernunterricht 1966*, Hamburg: Hamburger Fernlehrinstitut.

Dohmen, G. (1967) *Das Fernstudium. Ein neues pädagogisches Forschungs- und Arbeitsfeld*, Tübingen: DIFF.

Gough, E. (1984) 'Towards a philosophy of distance education', in K. Smith (ed.) *Diversity Down Under in Distance Education*, Toowoomba: Darling Downs Institute.

Graff, K. (1964) 'Briefwechsel und soziale Distanz', in *Epistolodidaktika* 1(1), 30–5.

Holmberg, B. (1960) *On the Methods of Teaching by Correspondence*, Lund: Gleerup.

Holmberg, B. (1981) *Status and Trends of Distance Education*,

London: Kogan Page.

Kaye, A. and Rumble, G. (1981) *Distance Teaching for Higher and Adult Education*, London: Croom Helm.

Moore, M. (1973) 'Towards a theory of independent learning and teaching', *Journal of Higher Education* 44: 666-78.

Peters, O. (1965) Der Fernunterricht. Basel: Weinheim.

Peters, O. (1971a) Theoretical aspects of correspondence instruction, in O. Mackenzie and E.L. Christensen (eds) *The Changing World of Correspondence Study*, University Park: Pennsylvania State University.

Peters, O. (1971b) *Texte zum Hochschulfernstudium*, Weinheim: Beltz.

Peters, O. (1973) *Die didaktische Struktur des Fernunterichts. Untersuchungen zu einer industrialisierten Form des Lehrens und Lernens*, Weinheim: Beltz.

Rebel, K-H. (1971) 'Die Funkkollegs der Quadriga', *Fernsehen und Bildung* 3: 185-94.

Ruggles, R. *et al.* (1982) *Learning at a Distance and the New Technology*, Vancouver: ERIBC.

Rumble, G. (1986) *The Planning and Management of Distance Education*, London: Croom Helm.

Rumble, G. and Keegan, D. (1982) 'General characteristics of the distance teaching universities', in G. Rumble and K. Harry (eds) *The Distance Teaching Universities*, London: Croom Helm, pp. 204-24.

Sewart, D. (1978) 'Continuity of concern for students in a system of learning at a distance', *Ziff Papiere 22*, Hagen: Fernuniversität.

Sewart, D. (1983) 'Editorial', *ICDE Bulletin* 1:5.

Sparkes, J.J. (1980) *Feedback Theory* (Technology Foundation Course Unit No. 1), Milton Keynes: Open University.

Sparkes, J. (1983) 'The problem of creating a discipline of distance education', *Distance Education* 4(2), 197-205.

Wedemeyer, C. (1963) 'Problems in learning by correspondence', in *The Brandenburg Memorial Essays on Correspondence Instruction*, Madison: University of Wisconsin.

Wedemeyer, C. (1981) *Learning at the Back-door*, Madison: University of Wisconsin.

Chapter Two

OPEN, NON-TRADITIONAL, AND DISTANCE EDUCATION

When we studied the research in education we read, for example, that ... 'the word instruction refers to the activity which takes place during schooling, and within the CLASSROOM setting'. It was clear that a vast number of adult learners were receiving instruction in non-group settings, and we concluded that educational theory which did not provide a place for such learning and teaching was incomplete, and unsatisfactory.

Michael G. Moore, 1971

BACKGROUND

When the research reported in this book began, analysis of distance education was characterized by confusion over terminology and by lack of precision on what areas of education were being discussed or what was being excluded. The confusion can be highlighted by listing the terms used in English for this field of education: 'correspondence study', 'home study', 'external studies', 'independent study', 'teaching at a distance', 'off-campus study', 'open learning', and there may well have been more. Allied to this was inconsistency about the boundaries that could be set to areas that had some similarities to distance education, either in philosophy or procedure, but which could not be identified with it. Among these areas of educational concern were: non-conventional education, extra-mural studies, educational broadcasting, non-traditional education, and the like.

The purpose of this chapter is to emphasize the importance of study of the non-conventional structures in education and then to provide a listing of the forms of non-conventional education which have similarities to distance education. The next chapter then attempts to define distance education in a

18

way which identifies it and isolates it for heuristic purposes from all other forms of education.

METHODOLOGY

The research began by the analysis of a very large grouping of institutions that had non-conventional or distance elements. The list included: public and private correspondence schools, rural development projects, educational broadcasting networks, open colleges and universities, external and distance departments of conventional institutions, universities without walls, extra-mural and external degree programmes, experiential learning, and other experimental structures.

The findings confirmed the results of an investigation of 'more than 2,000 items of literature pertaining to educational programmes in which learners were not in face-to-face relationships with teachers', carried out by Michael Moore at the University of Wisconsin a decade earlier. Moore presents the result of his investigation thus: 'Teaching consists of two families of activity with many characteristics in common, but different in one aspect so important that a theory explaining one cannot satisfactorily explain the other' (1977:5).

Moore (1977:6) describes his two families of educational activities as follows:

• The first of these families, the older, better understood, more fully researched, includes all educational situations where the teacher is physically contiguous with his students, so that the primary means of communication is his voice, and in which (to use the economists' terms) teaching is a 'service' that is 'consumed' simultaneously with its 'production'.

• The second family of teaching methods, and the subject of our concern, includes educational situations distinguished by the separation of the teacher from his learners, so that communication has to be facilitated by a mechanical or electronic medium. Teaching in this environment is 'consumed' at a time or place different from that at which it is 'produced', and to reach the learner it must be contained, transported, stored and delivered. There may be interaction, between learner and teacher, but if so, it is so greatly affected by the delay resulting from the necessity to communicate across distance or time, that it cannot be an assured component of teaching strategy, as it may in classroom or group

19

teaching. We refer to this as *Distance Teaching*.

CONVENTIONAL EDUCATION

Moore's 'first family of educational activities' is often referred to as 'conventional education'. Conventional education is the normal on-campus provision at school, college, or university level. For the purposes of this book the description provided by Kaye and Rumble is adequate: 'The term "conventional education" is applied to formal classroom-based instruction in a school, college or university setting, where teacher and students are physically present at the same time at the same place' (1979:22).

In educational literature this is regarded as the 'normal' form of educational provision and the complaint of Moore over a decade ago is that he had found hundreds of references of the type 'the word instruction refers to the activity which takes place *during* schooling, and *within* the *classroom* setting'. In distance education writing, one often finds the term 'face-to-face education' used for normal provision. In this study an attempt at further precision is made from time to time with the use of the term 'conventional, oral, group-based' education in place of 'face-to-face'.

As the research progressed it became clear that distance education and conventional education as defined by Kaye and Rumble could be established as two mutually exclusive categories and that the literature contained other major clusters of concepts that would repay further analysis. These were 'non-traditional education', 'indirect education', 'open education', and 'educational technology'.

NON-TRADITIONAL EDUCATION

The relationship between non-traditional education and distance education was addressed by Moore in the early 1970s. His decision (1973:661) to place distance education amongst the non-traditional forms of education is a far-reaching one. If accepted it would contribute to the fragility of this form of education and its continual lack of status in the eyes of many administrators and educationists in conventional institutions.

The presentation of 'non-traditional education' by the Carnegie Committee on Non-traditional Education was published as *Diversity by Design* (1973) under the editorship of Gould and may be considered comprehensive and authoritative. Gould acknowledges that the problem of 'How to define non-traditional study accurately and comprehensively was a stumbling block we never quite hurdled to our satisfaction'.

Gould (1973:5) presents the Committee's view of non-traditional education thus:

> Despite our lack of a completely suitable definition, we always seemed to sense the areas of education around which our interests centred. This community of concern was a mysterious light in the darkness, yet not at all mysterious in retrospect. Most of us agreed that non-traditional study is more an attitude than a system and thus can never be defined except tangentially. This attitude puts the student first and the institution second, concentrates more on the former's need than the latter's convenience, encourages diversity of individual opportunity rather than uniform prescription, and de-emphasises time, space, and even course requirements in favour of competence and, where applicable, performance.

For the purposes of this study, therefore, 'non-traditional learning' is a vast generalized term for a vague range of educational programmes that diverge from what is seen to be the norm.

INDIRECT OR MEDIATED EDUCATION

Education may be described as 'direct' or 'indirect' in accordance with the presence or absence of conventional, face-to-face communication. In the next chapter an attempt will be made to provide a definition of distance education, which will show that all the other forms of indirect education listed, either never possess all the characteristics of distance education as defined or else do so only on occasion - so that care is needed by researchers to indicate when they consider these educational possibilities as forming part of distance education and when they do not do so.

The diagram presented in Fig. 2.1, developed from an idea by Peters, may prove helpful to the reader in recognizing direct or indirect forms of education.

The various mediated forms of education in Fig. 2.1 all bear resemblances to distance education but lack one or more of the essential components of a distance education programme:

Figure 2.1 Relationship of distance education to other forms of indirect education

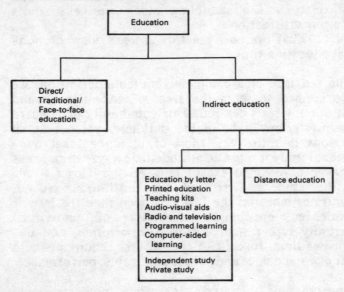

Source: Adapted and translated from Peters (1973)

- *Education by letter*. From Plato and Paul to Erasmus letters have been used for instructional purposes and the practice, doubtless, continues today. They lack the structuring of an educational institution that is a characteristic of distance education.
- *Printed education*. Pamphlets, books, and teach-yourself manuals fall into this category. The lack of an educational organization is again the major factor which distinguishes these from distance education, together with the impossibility of two-way communication. It is clear that many people learn a great deal from these means, even though they may lack didactical structuring or even an educational goal.
- *Teaching kits*. In increasing use in face-to-face teaching are kits of various kinds containing samples, games, and specimens on which students are invited to work without supervision.
- *Audio-visual aids*. When lecturers communicate with students by means of audio-visual aids: slides, film, audio, and videotapes, they are teaching indirectly. Although such aids can be used in distance education it is their use in face-to-face education that is in question here.

- *Radio and television.* Many people learn a great deal from radio and television and sometimes those media are used in distance education programmes. Kenneth Clarke's *Civilisation* or Jacob Bronowski's *The Ascent of Man* were not conceived as part of an education programme. Nevertheless they have become part of both on-campus and distance education programmes when offered for credit with accompanying didactically structured assignment, reading, and assessment materials.
- *Programmed learning*, is a form of indirect teaching which has many similarities to distance education. Both demand extensive preparation of learning materials, careful sequencing, and tend towards the individualizing of learning.
- *Computer-aided learning* is a form of indirect education and is used extensively in many conventional teaching programmes.

OPEN EDUCATION

There is extensive overlap between the use of the term 'open education' and distance education. The decision of the United Kingdom Government in the mid-1960s to rename the 'University of the Air' the 'Open University' popularized the term 'open'. It is found in the titles of the distance teaching universities in Pakistan, Sri Lanka, Thailand, and Venezuela, and in the titles of the multi-level distance colleges such as the Open Learning Institute of British Columbia and the Open College of Further Education of South Australia, both restructured in the 1980s.

The terms are not, however, synonymous. Writing from a Latin American background Escotet distinguishes them thus:

> *Open education* is particularly characterised by the removal of restrictions, exclusions and privileges; by the accreditation of students' previous experiences; by the flexibility of the management of the time variable; and by substantial changes in the traditional relationship between professors and students. On the other hand, *distance education* is a modality which permits the delivery of a group of didactic media without the necessity of regular class participation, where the individual is responsible for his own learning.
>
> (Escotet 1980:144)

Keegan and Rumble (1982:12) argue that the open universities should be termed 'distance teaching universities'. McKenzie *et al.* in their 1975 book *Open Learning* define 'open learning' as follows:

> Open learning is an imprecise phrase to which a range of meanings can be, and is, attached. It eludes definition. But as an inscription to be carried in procession on a banner, gathering adherents and enthusiasms, it has great potential. For its very imprecision enables it to accommodate many different ideas and aims.
>
> (McKenzie *et al.* 1975:21)

'Open' learning, therefore, is a term that is not to be used in an administrative context; its context is, rather, theoretical and describes, for instance, colleges with 'open' administration policies or a special spirit. Open learning can, in fact, be carried on under both face-to-face and distance conditions. Many of the distance teaching universities, for instance, have closed and rigid structures, are inflexible and slow to respond to community educational needs, have cut-off dates for computer-marked assignments and fixed assessment patterns. They design learning materials that narrow the curriculum and leave little room for interpretation outside the direction provided by the course designers.

Thus, while some basic ideas are shared by both open learning and distance education, the terms are not synonymous. 'We do not identify distance education with open learning', write Smith and Kelly (1987), 'in spite of the fact that terms like "open university" and "open campus programme" are in use world-wide. Institutions which adopt these titles usually lay claim to being open in terms of access and occasionally in terms of freedom from time constraints on students but in other ways they may be very closed.'

McKenzie *et al.* (1975:21) show that the two terms of the phrase 'open learning' carry with them emotional overtones that evoked a wide response in the 1950s and 1960s. Nearly a generation later, in the mid-1980s, there was a renewed interest in open learning in the UK (Lewis 1984; Freeman 1986; Grugeon 1987). This interest was characterized by government-initiated projects such as the Open Tech of the Manpower Services Commission and the government-backed Open College.

In a recent article Freeman traces the history of the phrase 'open' learning and underlines its tensions. 'The Open College started in 1963', he writes, 'when Michael Young and Brian

Jackson developed the idea of a high technology distance teaching system for the UK. NEC, the OU, Flexi-study, the CET OLS programme and the Open Tech Programme have led the way with so many different schemes. But we have never been able to create an approach which can provide a truly open system' (1986:6).

Deakin University provides a guideline for those who want to use the adjective 'open' in an administrative context. It indicates that it organizes three types of courses: 'on-campus', 'open campus', and 'off-campus'. It defines 'off-campus' as 'study not generally requiring attendance at the university. Course materials are posted and arrangements are made for students to sit examinations at specified centres' and states that 'open campus' is a mode of study which involves both on-campus and off-campus study (1988:viii).

Despite the interest in 'open' education and 'open' learning in the United States in the 1960s and in the UK in the mid-1980s, the term 'open education' remains hazardous if used in an administrative context.

EDUCATIONAL TECHNOLOGY

Educational technology plays an essential role in distance education. The term 'distance education', however, would become meaningless if it were forced to include all forms of educational technology or of education at a distance. The distinction between the field of educational technology and distance education is an important one. In educational technology the technology is usually a supplement to the teacher; in distance education it is usually a substitute for the teacher. Technology as a supplement to the teacher always makes the teaching more costly, in theory, than a teacher without technology. Educational technology in conventional education is normally used in classrooms or lecture theatres or specially constructed resource centres.

In distance education the technology may make the teaching either less costly or more costly (see Chapter 10) and may obviate the need for the provision of educational buildings and classrooms.

A working definition of educational technology would probably include both the use of technology 'in education' and technology 'of education'. Boyd suggests that 'educational technology is engaged in the task of choosing and deploying various forms of strategies, systems, programmes and machines to meet the educational needs and aspirations of our clients'

(1988:114).

Rigorously to be excluded from the concept 'distance education' are all uses of educational technology in classrooms, lecture theatres, or laboratories of conventional institutions, whether the technology is print-, audio-, video-, or computer-based, and where the technology is a supplement to and not a substitute for the teacher.

OTHER FORMS OF NON-TRADITIONAL EDUCATION

A final grouping of non-traditional educational structures is listed here as a preparation for the attempt to define 'distance education' in the following chapter. Some of these structures approximate closely to it.

- *Extension programmes* are ways of extending the expertise of a university or college to new populations. The term can imply offering the same programmes as for full-time, day-time students by different means, at different locations, or at different times. An *extra-mural* department usually has a similar function of extending the expertise of the university to a broader community.
- *Extended campus* refers to provision of lectures at alternative locations often far from the official campus.
- *University without walls* implies the design of an individualized programme based on a learning contract for students with clear learning objectives who cannot realize their whole educational aspirations through existing programmes. A university without walls programme can include experiential learning credits, ordinary lectures, distance education elements, learning from community sources, or job-related activities, all of which can be evaluated towards a college or university degree.
- *Experiential learning* programmes are those which give credit for prior learning which did not take place in a lecture room setting and was not sponsored by an education institution, but was acquired through work experience.
- *The external degree* is a degree programme which can be completed in the following manner: a student entering the programme with the minimum entrance qualification can complete it with less than 25 per cent of the required work taking the form of campus-based classroom instruction (Sosdian and Sharp 1977:1).

REFERENCES

Boyd, G. (1988) 'The impact of society on educational technology', *British Journal of Educational Technology* 105:116.

Deakin University (1988) *University Calendar*. Geelong: Deakin University.

Escotet, M. (1980) 'Adverse factors in the development of an open university in Latin America', *Programmed Learning and Educational Technology* 17(4): 262-70.

Freeman, R. (1986) 'Why do we need an Open College?' *OLS News* **19**.

Gould, S. (1973) *Diversity by Design*. San Francisco: Jossey Bass.

Grugeon, D. (1987) 'Editorial', *Open Learning* **2**(1):1.

Kaye, A. and Rumble, G. (1979) *An Analysis of Distance Teaching Systems*. Milton Keynes: Open University.

Keegan, D. and Rumble, G. (1982) 'Distance teaching at university level', in G. Rumble and K. Harry (eds) *The Distance Teaching Universities*, London: Croom Helm.

Lewis, R. (1984) *Open Learning in Action*, London: Council for Educational Technology

McKenzie, O., Postgate, R., and Scupham, J. (1975) *Open Learning*, Paris: UNESCO.

Moore, M. (1971) 'Teaching the distant adult learner', cited in D. Sewart, D. Keegan, and B. Holmberg, *Distance Education. International Perspectives*. London: Croom Helm.

Moore, M. (1971) 'Toward a theory of independent learning and teaching', *Journal of Higher Education* **44**: 661-79.

Moore, M. (1977) *On a Theory of Independent Study*, Hagen: Fernuniversität.

Peters, O. (1973) *Die didaktische Struktur des Fernunterrichts*, Weinheim: Beltz.

Smith, P. and Kelly, M. (eds) (1987) *Distance Education and the Mainstream*, London: Croom Helm.

Sosdian, C. and Sharp, L. (1977) *Guide to Undergraduate External Degree Programs in the US*. Washington: NIE.

Chapter Three

DEFINITION OF DISTANCE EDUCATION

It is natural for man to desire to know.

Aristotle, 323 BC

CONTEXT

The purpose of this chapter is to enable readers to make their way through the maze of terminology encountered in the literature, and to formulate a definition of that area of education under study that will form the basis for discussion in this book. The definition developed here is used as an instrument to eliminate from the discussion forms of education which are not the same as distance education although they may have similarities to it. The methodology used is based on the contributions of acknowledged experts in the field coupled with the use of feedback techniques.

One of the advantages of seeing educational research in the context of feedback techniques is that it solves the constant problem of which comes first: the research or the hypothesis? In feedback theory, investigation is seen as a loop process and one can commence at any appropriate point in the loop in the attempt to deepen knowledge and understanding.

A DESCRIPTION

The need to clarify terminology is immediate. No progress can be made in formulating the theoretical underpinnings of an area of educational endeavour or in developing guides to good practice if there is no agreement on the area of education under discussion.

This book proposes the adoption of 'distance education' as a generic term for the field of education under discussion.

It may be described thus: 'Distance education' is a generic term that includes the range of teaching/learning strategies referred to as 'correspondence education' or 'correspondence study' at further education level in the United Kingdom; as 'home study' at further education level and 'independent study' at higher educational level in the United States; as 'external studies' in Australia; and as 'distance teaching' or 'teaching at a distance' by the Open University of the United Kingdom. In French it is referred to as *'télé-enseignement'; Fernstudium/Fernunterricht* in German; *'educación a distancia'* in Spanish and *'teleducacão'* in Portuguese.

This description lists the major terms used by distance education institutions in the English-speaking world and gives parallel terms for the major European languages. 'Distance education' subsumes a number of existing terms but not all are synonymous.

Correspondence education/correspondence study

These terms have a long history in the education of children and adults at a distance. They still have their supporters who claim that nearly all distance education is still organized through the post and that both the public and prospective students recognize the terms.

'Correspondence education' is defined in the UNESCO volume *Terminology of Adult Education* as:

Education conducted by the postal services without face-to-face contact between teacher and learner. Teaching is done by written or tape-recorded materials sent to the learner, whose progress is monitored through written or taped exercises to the teacher, who corrects them and returns them to the learner with criticisms and advice.

(UNESCO 1979)

The main problem with the term 'correspondence education' is that it cannot encompass the didactic potential of this form of education in the 1980s and beyond: print-, audio-, video-, and computer-based possibilities must be reflected by the terminology chosen. Another problem is that critics of the term tend to associate 'correspondence education' and 'correspondence study' with some of the less successful aspects of distance education in the past and to feel that these terms contribute to the still-questioned status of study at a distance in many countries.

The concept of distance education

Even when distance education is print-based, the term 'correspondence education' is inadequate to describe courses by newspaper or systems with no postal component.

A term is, however, needed to designate the postal subgroup of the print-based forms of distance education in which student contact is not encouraged. It seems suitable to reserve the term 'correspondence education' for this purpose.

Home study

Communications theory experts tell us that words grow tired and if they do, then 'correspondence study' is a tired word. It is significant that as early as 1926 when the directors of the correspondence schools of the United States came together to form an association, the title chosen was the National Home Study Council and not the National Correspondence Study Council.

'Home study', however, has little claim to being an overall term as it is used mainly in the United States and is there confined to further education (technical and vocationally orientated institutions) and not higher education (universities and university-orientated colleges). In addition, the distance student may not, in fact, study at home or may study in part at home and in part at other centres.

Independent study

The proponent of 'independent study' as an overall term for this area of education was Charles A. Wedemeyer, formerly of the University of Wisconsin at Madison. Wedemeyer considered that 'Independent study in the American context is generic for a range of teaching-learning activities that sometimes go by separate names (correspondence study, open education, radio-television teaching, individualised learning)' (1977:2115).

This term is often used for distance education programmes at higher education level in the US (Markowitz 1983). Its weakness is that it indicates the independence from an educational institution and this is not the case in distance education. Even in the US there is hesitancy about using the term as it is often used for individual study programmes containing periods of normal lectures organized on a contract basis agreed to by a student and a faculty member.

External studies

External studies is the term most widely used in Australia. It describes well the ethos of distance education as found in Australian universities and colleges of advanced education: a form of education that is 'external to' but not 'separated from' the faculty staff of the institution. The same staff have two groups of students, one on-campus, the other external, and they prepare both groups for the same examinations and awards.

However, 'external studies' can have little claim to general acceptance because of its limitation to Australia and because of possible confusion with programmes structured differently, such as the American external degree (see Chapter 2).

Distance teaching or teaching at a distance

These two terms have been used as a characteristic of this form of education for over a decade. Moore described 'distance teaching' as:

All those teaching methods in which, because of the physical separation of learners and teachers, the interactive (stimulation, explanation, questioning, guidance) as well as the preactive phase of teaching (selecting objectives, planning curriculum and instructional strategies), is conducted through print, mechanical or electronic devices.
(Moore 1973:669)

The term has grown greatly in popularity since the inception of the Open University (UK) which used it for its journal, *Teaching at a Distance*. It is, nevertheless, inadequate for the field of education we want to define. Just as 'distance learning' would be too student-based as an overall term and would tend to ignore the role of the institution, so 'distance teaching' is too teacher-orientated and places all the emphasis on the institution.

Distance education

Distance teaching and distance learning are each only half the process we are seeking to describe. 'Distance teaching' indicates clearly the process of course development by which a distance institution prepares learning materials for students.

In the same way wide currency has been given to the term 'distance learning' or 'learning at a distance' for the process as seen from the student's perspective.

There is a peculiar necessity in distance systems that the perspective of student learning should be encompassed within the term chosen. 'Distance teaching' often does not teach. Costly distance teaching materials, prepared over months and sometimes years, often lie unopened and discarded in the homes of prospective students. The essential intersubjectivity that has often been seen as the essence of the education process has not occurred.

'Distance education' is a suitable term to bring together both the teaching and learning elements of this field of education. The relationship of 'distance teaching' and 'distance learning' may be illustrated as shown in Fig. 3.1.

Figure 3.1 Relationship of distance teaching to distance education

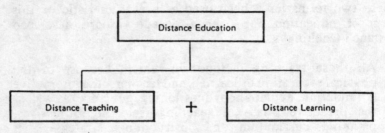

Over a decade ago Rawson-Jones summed up the pros and cons of the term:

> I do not like the term 'distance education'. It seems to put an undue emphasis on the distance between the teacher and the learner. But I cannot think of a better name for a multi-media educational process in which the teacher and the students may never meet in a face-to-face situation. 'Distance teaching' seems too teacher-oriented and 'distance learning' too student-based. Distance education combines the two, so, in the absence of a better name for the process, I shall use it when appropriate.
>
> (Rawson-Jones 1974:61)

Since then the term has gained in strength and acceptance. It indicates well the basic characteristic of this form of education: the separation of teacher and learner which distinguishes it from conventional, oral, group-based education. It also encompasses well the two characteristic operating systems which later in this study will be shown to be unique to distance education: the course development subsystem (distance teaching) and a student support subsystem (distance learning).

It is also a term for the future. Distance educators in the past have held on to terms like 'correspondence' or 'home study' because, it was claimed, they were comforting to students. There is every evidence that citizens of the late 1980s and 1990s will be able to cope with distance in a way previous generations could never dream of. Students, too, are coming to choose distance rather than backing off from it.

Perhaps the main problem with the term is that it tends to mask the fact that most students in distance systems are metropolitan residents. Only in Australia, Canada, and some developing countries does distance education belie its urban origins in the UK, Sweden, Germany, and the United States to embrace vast distances – and even in Australia and Canada 50-70 per cent of enrolments are normally from the major cities. However, it is the distance between the teaching acts and the learning acts that is crucial, not the magnitude of the geographical separation of teacher and learner.

In this chapter 'distance education' is chosen as the most suitable term for this form of education and it is proposed as the only term for international usage. Terms that are considered synonymous with or constituents of it were considered earlier in this chapter; terms for fields of education or educational strategies that are similar to it but not to be regarded as synonymous with it were considered in Chapter 2.

Terms such as 'correspondence study/education', 'distance teaching' or 'teaching at a distance' will be used to refer to subsets of distance education or to specific elements such as the course development part of the process. 'Home study' becomes an American equivalent of 'distance education at further education level' and 'independent study' the American term for 'distance education at higher education level', with 'external studies' being a term suitable for the particular Australian structures.

LANGUAGES OTHER THAN ENGLISH

'Distance education' is the normal equivalent of the French *télé-enseignement* (teaching from a distance) and the earlier *enseignement par correspondence* (teaching by correspondence). In the mid-1980s French terminology changed and reflected the acceptance of 'distance education' in English. The French Government changed the name of the *Centre National de Télé-enseignement* (National Centre for Teaching from a Distance) to *Centre National d'Enseignement à Distance* (National Centre for Distance Teaching) and in Canada the *Comité pour l'Education à distance du Conseil des Universités d'Ontario* used a direct translation (*Education à distance*) of 'distance education'.

'Distance education' is a satisfactory translation for both *Fernstudium* (distance study) and *Fernunterricht* (distance teaching) in German, though in some circumstances it may be necessary to translate *Fernstudium* as 'distance education at higher education level' and *Fernunterricht* as 'distance education at further education level' because of the awkward status problems between the two terms in the Federal Republic of Germany, where the word *Studium* is usually reserved specifically for study at university level.

In usage the split often seems to be '*Fernstudium*' for publicly sponsored distance education and '*Fernunterricht*' when distance education is privately conducted. This problem does not exist in the German Democratic Republic where *Fernstudium* is used interchangeably both for the higher education programmes at a distance organized from the *Zentralstelle für das Hochschulfern-Studium des Ministeriums für Hoch- und Fachschulwesen* in Dresden and for the technological education programmes from a similar institute in Karl-Marx-Stadt.

'Distance education' is the correct term for translating *educación a distancia* which has emerged as the dominant term in Spanish. It appears in the titles of the two open universities, Universidad Nacional de Educación a Distancia in Madrid and the Universidad Estatal a Distancia in Costa Rica.

A DEFINITION OF DISTANCE EDUCATION

A clear idea of what is the subject of discussion is essential in a book on an area of study in which there has been much confusion about terminology. A clear definition is also important in the rather ill-defined areas of non-traditional education, open education, and non-conventional education. It is important to be able to say whether distance education is to be regarded as the same as or different from university without walls, extra-mural studies, experiential learning, off-campus education, open learning, extended campus, the American external degree, or university extension.

The rest of this chapter seeks to establish a definition of distance education which will serve as a basis for the analysis in the rest of the book.

A satisfactory framework for definition in education is provided by the American educational philosopher Scheffler (1968), who presented the scheme shown in Fig. 3.2 for different types of definition. Scheffler sees scientific definitions as being based on special knowledge which is used to construct a network of theory adequate to all available facts encompassed in the definition, whereas general definitions are statements that a given term is to be understood in a certain way for the space of some discussions or for several discussions.

Figure 3.2 Types of definition in education

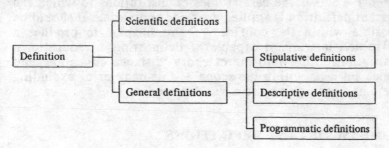

Source: Adapted from Scheffler (1968)

He claims there are three types of general definitions: stipulative, descriptive, and programmatic. Stipulative definitions state that a given term is to be taken as equivalent to some other given term within a particular context. This is not the type of definition needed here as a stipulative definition does not claim to reflect the previously accepted usage of the defined terms. A general descriptive definition answers the question 'What does that term mean?'. It not only serves as a convention for usage in discussion but also always explains the defined terms by giving an account of its prior usage. A programmatic definition is a definition with a purpose, a programme: it seeks to include additional items within a term or to exclude from a term elements which people had previously thought were included. There are elements of the programmatic in many definitions of distance education, especially if it is claimed that all such systems are flexible, open, and use all sorts of modern communications technology.

In Scheffler's terms this study commences with a general descriptive definition and seeks to proceed by feedback and refinement towards a scientific definition.

It seems appropriate to begin with a search of the literature for authoritative or accepted definitions and to analyse them for their common elements. Distance education, however, has a 100 year history and the elements of a definition that can be established by this process do not therefore exist as abstractions; they must correspond to the reality.

It is correct therefore to examine the definition in the context of existing institutions, then to consider more recent definitions before re-examining the definition established in the light of existing institutions. The process is then continued: it is cyclic and continuous. If the search of the literature is extensive and if the case studies of institutions to which the nascent definition is applied are wide and varied, it should be possible within the confines of this chapter to produce a definition instrument capable of delineating all educational institutions either into the category 'distance education' and hence subjects within the scope of this book or of excluding them and consigning them to other studies.

SOME IMPORTANT DEFINITIONS

G. Dohmen (1967)

The first definition is chosen from Dohmen, a director of the German Distance Education Institute (DIFF) at Tübingen in the Federal Republic of Germany:

> Distance education (*Fernstudium*) is a systematically organised form of self-study in which student counselling, the presentation of learning material and the securing and supervising of students' success is carried out by a team of teachers, each of whom has responsibilities. It is made possible at a distance by means of media which can cover long distances. The opposite of 'distance education' is 'direct education' or 'face-to-face education': a type of education that takes place with direct contact between lecturers and students.
>
> (Dohmen 1967:9)

From this early formulation may be highlighted:

- the organization of self study by an institution;
- use of media; and
- differences from direct contact between lecturers and students.

O. Peters (1973)

Distance teaching/education (*Fernunterricht*) is a method of imparting knowledge, skills and attitudes which is rationalised by the application of division of labour and organisational principles as well as by the extensive use of technical media, especially for the purpose of reproducing high quality teaching material which makes it possible to instruct great numbers of students at the same time wherever they live. It is an industrialised form of teaching and learning.

(Peters 1973:206)

Characteristic of Peters' position are:

- the use of technical media;
- the mass education of students at a distance; and
- the industrialization of the teaching process.

M. Moore (1973)

This definition is presented in 1973 and repeated without modification in 1977:

Distance teaching may be defined as the family of instructional methods in which the teaching behaviours are executed apart from the learning behaviours, including those that in a contiguous situation would be performed in the learner's presence, so that communication between the teacher and the learner must be facilitated by print, electronic, mechanical or other devices.

(Moore 1973:664; 1977:8)

Central to Moore's position are:

- the separation of teacher and learner; and
- the use of technical media.

B. Holmberg (1977)

> The term 'distance education' covers the various forms of study at all levels which are not under the continuous, immediate supervision of tutors present with their students in lecture rooms or on the same premises, but which, nevertheless, benefit from the planning, guidance and tuition of a tutorial organisation.
>
> (Holmberg 1977:9)

Basic to Holmberg's definition are two elements both of which can be considered essential:

- the separation of teacher and learner; and
- the planning of an educational organization.

The separation of teacher and learner is fundamental to all forms of distance education whether they be print-based, audio/radio-based, video/television-based, or computer-based. This separation differentiates distance education from all forms of conventional, face-to-face, direct teaching and learning.

The structuring of learning materials and the linking of these learning materials to effective learning by students through an educational organization differentiates distance education from private study, learning from interesting books or cultural television programmes.

TOWARDS A SYNTHESIS

In an article published in 1980 'On defining distance education' (Keegan 1980) a number of similar definitions were brought together and analysed. Six basic defining elements of distance education were proposed:

- the separation of teacher and learner which distinguishes it from face-to-face lecturing;
- the influence of an educational organization which distinguishes it from private study;
- the use of technical media, usually print, to unite teacher and learner and carry the educational content;
- the provision of two-way communication so that the student may benefit from or even initiate dialogue;
- the possibility of occasional meetings for both didactic and socialization purposes; and

- the participation in an industrialized form of education which, if accepted, contains the genus of radical separation of distance education from other forms within the educational spectrum.

The publication of this definition in 1980 led to extensive citation and feedback. In some cases (Peruniak 1983:66; Store 1981:171) it seemed that the definition was accepted as the basis for further research; in others commentary was provided which might lead to further precision. Further analysis and case studies of existing institutions led to the considerations which follow.

The separation of teacher and learner

An analysis of the definitions given in this chapter shows that the separation of teacher and learner is central to nearly all of them. This characteristic distinguishes distance education from conventional, oral, group-based education. Both the general public and educational writers appear to coincide in their acceptance of the separation of teacher and learner as a central characteristic of this form of education. An examination of institutions revealed various levels of separation, in which contact could range from nil, to voluntary, to compulsory. 'Quasi-permanent separation throughout the length of the learning process' was finally chosen as a suitable overall summing up of the mean of practice.

The role of the educational organization

It is important to delineate distance education not only from what happens in lecture theatres and classrooms but also from private study at home. Distance education is an institutionalized offering through public or private providers. This may be represented schematically as shown in Fig. 3.3. It is clear that people learn a lot throughout their lives, generally away from teachers and educational institutions. This may be from private reading, from TV, from attending a talk, from a friend, or in a thousand different ways. Distance education is an institutionalized form of provision. It shares with private study the individualized and private nature of study outside the structures of the learning group and at the same time has much of the administrative characteristics of institutionalized education on-campus.

Figure 3.3 Institutionalized and non-institutionalized learning

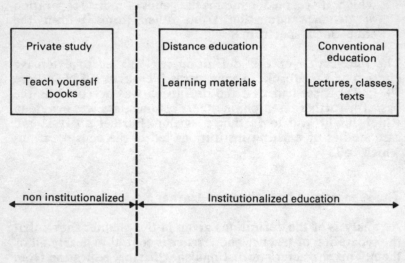

Fieldwork in distance institutions shows that the entry of an educational bureaucracy into what appears to be a private form of education is not always without trauma.

The pace of the technological medium (media)

In conventional systems the content of the course, especially that part that is not contained in recommended textbooks, is communicated by the teacher mainly by word of mouth - though it is clear that from primary school through to university the amount of self-study in project work and from textbooks may gradually increase. Distance education shatters this interpersonal communication and replaces it with some form of mechanical or electronic communication: print, telephone, teleconference, audio, video, broadcasting, computer. All of the communication has to take place by the use of one of a number of technological media.

Many years ago Delling (1966:173) called this element in a distance system the 'signal-carrier' and because of the diversity of procedures involved, careful formulation is needed of the role of the technological media in a definition of distance education.

Two-way communication

A definition of distance education needs to distinguish it from educational technology with which it is often confused. This can be accomplished neatly by defining two-way communication as essential in distance education and showing its absence in educational technology.

It is important that the student in a distance system can profit from dialogue with the institution that provides the learning materials; the student should be able to initiate this dialogue and not be just the recipient of it. Two-way communication is *not* provided by the publishers of textbooks nor even of do-it-yourself books. Two-way communication is *not* possible with educational television or radio programmes like *Sesame Street* or 'Learn French at home by radio' nor even by video- or audio-cassettes produced as resource materials for lecture or classroom use.

The separation of learner and the learning group

In the 1980 definition the 'possibility of occasional seminars' was listed as one of the constituents of a definition of distance education. In the light of feedback and further research it has been found necessary to restructure this formulation. Some definitions of distance education and an earlier form of the one being developed in this chapter tended to emphasize 'the teaching of students as individuals' and the importance of individualization in this form of education. Comparative research carried on after the publication of the 1980 definition, however, showed the survival in certain Scandinavian countries of group-based distance education (Edström 1970). The presentation of individualization in the formulation of the definitions had, therefore, to be modified, as a prerequisite for the methodology adopted was that *all* the evidence should be reflected.

Further feedback from Garrison and Shale (1987:9) and Sparkes (1987:237) made it important to emphasize the role in distance education of electronic groupings of students, by audio conferencing, teleconferencing, and computer conferences, in addition to the physical groupings reported by Edström.

It became clearer, moreover, that a focus on the study situation of the student was central to the concept of distance education. Some formula had to be found to reflect both the individualization of the distance student and the practice of institutions of providing either no, or voluntary, or compulsory face-to-face sessions. The reason for this is that in most conventional educational institutions one has to join a learning group or class if one wants to enrol in a course. The presence of the learning group is as fundamental a characteristic of conventional education as the timetabling of classes so that the teacher and student can be present in the same place and at the same time.

Distance education is different in that it does not compel the student to join the learning group in order to study. Most distance systems treat the student basically as an individual; group work may be compulsory, optional, or may never occur, depending on the structure of the distance system in which one enrols.

The advantages and disadvantages of the absence of the learning group in distance education is a practically untouched area for future research, though Sewart (1980:171) and Cropley and Kahl (1983:30) have alluded to this feature. Together with the separation of the learner from the teacher, the separation of the learner from the learning group throughout the length of the learning process is a characteristic feature of this form of education which distinguishes it from conventional, oral, group-based education.

Industrialization

The 1980 definition incorporated as an inherent characteristic an evaluation of Peters' industrialization theory. This decision was made after an analysis of the hundreds of institutional case studies presented by Peters in his study of distance education at technological and further education levels (Peters 1965) and at higher education level (Peters 1968) in all countries of the world plus the analysis undertaken by the author of the same or other institutions.

Reaction has been mixed. Some commentators, especially those writing from a management or administrative perspective (Rumble 1986) consider that Peters has provided a valuable insight. Others (Bååth 1981; Willén 1981) have hesitated at the harshness of Peters' terminology and doubted whether his concept of industrialization can be applied to all distance systems, especially small correspondence schools.

As a result of these considerations, the definition had by 1983 evolved to the following formulation:

Distance education is that field of educational endeavour

in which the learner is quasi-permanently separated from the teacher throughout the length of the learning process; the learner is quasi-permanently separated from the learning group throughout the length of the learning process; a technological medium replaces the interpersonal communication of conventional, oral, group-based education; the teaching/learning process is institutionalised (thus distinguishing it from Teach-yourself programmes); two-way communication is possible for both student and teacher (thus distinguishing it from other forms of educational technology). It represents an industrialisation of the educational process.

(Keegan 1983:503)

It can be seen that the support for industrialization as a component of distance education remains unchanged; it has, however, been moved outside the definition proper.

PRIVATIZATION

Early definitions of distance education, especially those of Wedemeyer and Moore tended to emphasize the independence, autonomy, and freedom of the distance learner. A recent definition by Gough of Deakin University reflects this tradition:

Distance education is a means of providing learning experiences for students through the use of self-instructional materials and access to educational resources, the use of which is largely determined by the student and which allow the student, for the most part, to choose the time, place and circumstances of learning.

(Gough 1981:10)

There are excellent elements in this definition but when it is compared with the reality of existing systems, it can be shown to have elements of Sheffler's programmatic type of definition in it. It proposes a programme, an ideal - many systems in fact do not promote learner autonomy in the way this definition would wish. Sharp cut-off dates for tutor-marked assignments (TMAs) and computer-marked assignments (CMAs), rigidity of content of learning materials, and inflexible learning structures are all too common in distance systems.

Independence, therefore, is not the element that the definition should reflect. The term 'privatization' is much closer to the reality. A distance system takes the student from the learning group and places him/her in a more private situation. Learning is often private when it is not institutionalized. Distance education is characterized by the privatization of institutional learning (Smith 1987:30).

CONCLUSION

In the light of these considerations the following definition of distance education is proposed.

Distance education is a form of education characterized by

- the quasi-permanent separation of teacher and learner throughout the length of the learning process (this distinguishes it from conventional face-to-face education);
- the influence of an educational organization both in the planning and preparation of learning materials and in the provision of student support services (this distinguishes it from private study and teach-yourself programmes);
- the use of technical media - print, audio, video or computer - to unite teacher and learner and carry the content of the course;
- the provision of two-way communication so that the student may benefit from or even initiate dialogue (this distinguishes it from other uses of technology in education); and
- the quasi-permanent absence of the learning group throughout the length of the learning process so that people are usually taught as individuals and not in groups, with the possibility of occasional meetings for both didactic and socialization purposes.

The definition seeks to take up the middle ground between the extremes of defining distance education so narrowly that it becomes an abstraction which does not correspond to existing reality, or so broadly that it becomes meaningless.

An example of a definition that is so narrow that it is not helpful in practice is that provided in the UNESCO study:

Distance education: 'Education conducted through the postal services, radio, television, telephone or newspaper, without face-to-face contact between teacher and learner. Teaching is done by specially prepared material transmitted to individuals or learning groups. Learners' progress is monitored through written or taped exercises, sent to the teacher, who corrects them and returns them to learners with criticism and advice'.

(UNESCO 1979:21)

Comparative studies of distance systems show that the element of face-to-face contact may be either non-existent, compulsory, or voluntary. The volume of face-to-face contact that would be consistent with the definition adopted for this study is indicated by the phrase 'the quasi-permanent separation of the learner from the teacher and from the learning group throughout the length of the learning process'.

Too vague a definition would be equally faulty. The range of 'education at a distance' is vast and comprises both distance education as defined here and a range of other resource-based teaching and learning strategies. If the confusion of the past is to be avoided and if the goal of this study is to be achieved (the identification of a discrete area of educational activity in such a way that it can provide a basis for other scholars to build a valid theoretical structure and guides to good practice), then to be excluded from the concept of distance education are:

- the use of printed, audio-based, video-based, or computer-based learning materials in classroom, lecture theatres, seminars, tutorial, and laboratory sessions for on-campus programmes;
- the use of printed, audio-based, video-based learning materials and computers in private study.

REFERENCES

Aristotle (323BC) *Nichomachaen Ethics*, 1.1.

Bååth, J. (1981) 'On the nature of distance education', *Distance Education* 2(2), 212-13.

Cropley, A. and Kahl, T. (1983) 'Distance education and distance learning: some psychological considerations', *Distance Education* 4(1)27-39.

Delling, R.M. (1966) 'Versuch der Grundlegung zu einer systematischen Theorie des Fernunterricht', in L. Sroka (ed.) *Fernunterricht 1966, Festschrift zum 50 Geburtstag von Walter Schultz-Rahe*, Hamburg: Hamburger Fernlehrinstitut.

Dohmen, G. (1967) *Das Fernstudium, Ein neues pädagogisches Forschungs-und Arbeitsfeld*, Tübingen: DIFF.

Edström, L. *et al.* (1970) *Mass Education: Studies in Adult Education and Teaching by Correspondence in Some Developing Countries*, Stockholm: Almquist & Wiksell.

Garrison, D. and Shale, D. (1987) 'Mapping the boundaries of distance education: problems in defining the field', *The American Journal of Distance Education* 1(1), 4-13.

Gough, E. (1981) 'Distance education at Deakin University and University Sains Malaysia', *Open Campus* 3(1), 10-15.

Holmberg, B. (1977) *Distance Education: A Survey and Bibliography*, London: Kogan Page.

Keegan, D. (1980) 'On defining distance education', *Distance Education* 1(1), 13-36.

Keegan, D. (1983) Review of Daniel *et al. Learning at a Distance. A World Perspective, International Review of Education* 29(4), 501-3.

Markowitz, H. (1983) 'Independent study by correspondence in American universities', *Distance Education* 4(2), 149-70.

Moore, M.G. (1973) 'Toward a theory of independent learning and teaching', *Journal of Higher Education* 44, 66-679.

Moore, M.G. (1977) *On a Theory of Independent Study*, Hagen: Fernuniversität (DIFF).

Peruniak, G. (1983) 'Interactive perspectives in distance education: a case study', *Distance Education* 4(1), 64-89.

Peters, O. (1965) *Der Fernunterricht*, Weinheim: Beltz.

Peters, O. (1968) *Das Hochschulfernstudium*, Weinheim: Beltz.

Peters, O. (1973) *Die didaktische Struktur der Fernunterrichts*, Weinheim & Basel: Beltz.

Rawson-Jones, K. (1974) 'Some trends in distance education', *Epistolodidaktika* 1, 67-8.

Rumble, G. (1986) *The Planning and Management of Distance Education*, London: Croom Helm.

Sewart, D. (1980) 'Creating an information base for an individualized support system in distance education', *Distance Education* 1(2), 171-87.

Sheffler, I. (1968) *The Philosophy of Education*, New York: Wiley.

Smith, P. (1987) 'Distance education and educational change', in P. Smith and M. Kelly (eds) *Distance Education and the Mainstream*, London: Croom Helm.

Sparkes, J. (1987) Book review. *Studies in Higher Education* 12(2), 237-8.

Store, R. (1981) 'An analysis of student responses in distance education systems', *British Journal of Educational Technology* 171-96.

UNESCO (1979) *Terminology of Adult Education/Termino-*

logie de la Educación de Adultos/Terminologie de l'Education des Adultes*, Paris: Ibedata.

Wedemeyer, C.A. (1977) 'Independent study', in A.S. Knowles (ed.) *The International Encyclopedia of Higher Education*, Boston: Northeastern University.

Willén, B. (1981) *Distance Education at Swedish Universities*, Stockholm: Almqvist & Wiksell.

Part II

THEORIES OF DISTANCE EDUCATION

Chapter Four

INDEPENDENCE AND AUTONOMY

> It is unfortunately true that the failure of correspondence
> study to develop a theory related to the mainstream of
> educational thought and practice has seriously handicapped
> the development and recognition of this field.
>
> Charles A. Wedemeyer, 1974

INTRODUCTION

Early pioneers of correspondence education, William Rainey
Harper of Chicago, William H. Lightly of Wisconsin, and Hans
Hermod of Malmö, wrote with verve and enthusiasm about the
advantages and disadvantages of this form of education. But
the historian of distance education, Rudolf Manfred Delling
from Tübingen, claimed in 1966 that although institutionalized
distance education had existed for about 100 years, it was only
during the last few years that the practice of distance teaching
had commenced to rely on theory. Nevertheless there was no
systematic theory of distance education which might make it
possible to classify practitioners' individual experiences in
relation to their essence (1966:183). Delling states that the first
theoretical work was developed in the 1950s. In 1959 the East
German scholar Joannes Riechert, of Freiburg, published a
book *Schreiben, Lehren und Verstehen (Write, Teach and
Learn)*, and at about the same time from Sweden came an
international description of the field *On the Methods of
Teaching by Correspondence* by Börje Holmberg (1960). This
was translated into German in 1962.

When theoretical approaches began to emerge in the 1970s,
their development was fitful. The first major theoretical
structure, and to date the most comprehensive (Peters, 1973),
categorized distance education as an industrialization of the
education process and suggested that the closest parallel to a

distance teaching organization was the industrialized production of goods. A mail order firm would have a structure similar to an institution for this form of education.

The claim of Wedemeyer that distance education has failed 'to develop a theory related to the mainstream of educational thought and practice' remains true today. The following chapters attempt a detailed analysis of the theoretical approaches that have been attempted to date. They are presented here because they are among the best available in the literature and because it is correct to present a detailed exposé of the work of previous writers before attempting to suggest a new basis for theoretical structure. Nascent, if fragile, theoretical proposals have been found in the writings of Moore, Peters, and Holmberg; ideas of value have been contributed by Delling, Wedemeyer, Bååth, Daniel, Smith, and Sewart.

For the purposes of this book the more important positions formulated to date are classified into three groupings:

* *Theories of autonomy and independence.* These contributions come mainly from the late 1960s and early 1970s and the major representatives are Rudolf Manfred Delling (FRG), Charles A. Wedemeyer (USA) and Michael G. Moore (USA) (Chapter 4).
* *Theory of industrialization.* Otto Peters' work in the Federal Republic of Germany comprised comparative studies throughout the 1960s and theoretical formulation in the early 1970s (Chapter 5).
* *Theories of interaction and communication.* More contemporary views from Börje Holmberg (Sweden/Federal Republic of Germany), John A. Bååth (Sweden), David Sewart (UK), Kevin C. Smith (Australia), and John S. Daniel (Canada) (Chapter 6).

A HELPING ORGANIZATION

Rudolf Manfred Delling of the Deutsches Institut für Fernstudien an der Universität Tübingen is a historian and bibliographer. In 1966 he provided this definition:

Distance education (*Fernunterricht*) is a planned and systematic activity which comprises the choice, didactic preparation and presentation of teaching materials as well as the supervision and support of student learning and which is achieved by bridging the physical distance between student and teacher by means of at least one appropriate technical medium.

(Delling 1966:186)

Delling sees distance education as a multi-dimensional system of learning and communication processes, with the aid of an artificial signal-carrier. In many of his writings (1968, 1978) he lists eight dimensions:

* a learner
* society (including legislation, administration, family, etc.)
* a helping organization (distance teaching institutions)
* a learning objective
* the content to be learned
* the result of learning
* distance
* a signal-carrier

Remarkable in his approach are his hesitation to label distance education a teaching process (distance colleges or departments are organizations which 'help' learning) and the absence of the teacher from the eight dimensions of the system.

A distance education course is an artificial, dialogic opportunity for learning in which the distance between the learner and the helping organization is bridged by an artificial signal-carrier.

From the start the concepts of feedback and two-way communication are central to Delling's position. He sees an essential difference between learning opportunities that are *monologues* (books, newspapers, journals, documentary films, lectures without discussion, broadcasts, self-teaching courses, and other self-instructional material) and those that are *dialogic* (normal classroom or school teaching, conversations, letters with answers, and distance education courses). Monologues are based on one-way communication, whereas dialogues are characterized by two-way communication.

The world of distance education, he claims, has little of the characteristics of 'teaching' because there is, in general, no teacher in the system and the functions relating to student learning within the helping organization are performed by a variety of machines, people, and materials.

Delling tends to reduce the role of the teacher and of the educational organization to a minimum and throw the whole emphasis on the autonomy and independence of the learner. This is especially important because adults are normally the learners in distance programmes. Adults do not, he suggests, accept the conventional educator-pupil relationship. The function of the 'helping organization' is to take over, upon the wish of learners, everything that they cannot yet do for themselves, with the tendency that the learners eventually become autonomous. When this occurs the only function left for the helping organization is to provide information, documentation, and library facilities.

Delling seems to want to place distance education outside the field of educational theory. He sees it falling within the range of communication processes and to be characterized by industrialized mechanisms which carry on its artificial dialogic and two-way communication processes. He reduces to a minimum the role of the teacher and throws the whole weight of his analysis on the learning of the student studying at a distance.

INDEPENDENT STUDY

The term 'independent study' was used by Charles A. Wedemeyer to describe distance education at university level. For much of his professional life he was Professor of Education at the University of Wisconsin, Madison and closely associated with the Independent Study Division of the National University Extension Association of the United States of America.

He uses the term 'independent study' to describe distance education at university level and gives this definition:

> 'Independent learning' is that learning, that changed behaviour, that results from activities carried on by learners in space and time, learners whose environment is different from that of the school, learners who may be guided by teachers but who are not dependent upon them, learners who accept degrees of freedom and responsibility in initiating and carrying out the activities that lead to learning.
>
> (Wedemeyer 1973:73)

Wedemeyer's thought is generous and liberal. A major influence is the philosophy of Carl Rogers. There are two bases for his views on independent study: a democratic social ideal and a liberal educational philosophy. He considers that nobody should be denied the opportunity to learn because he is poor, geographically isolated, socially disadvantaged, in poor health, institutionalized, or otherwise unable to place himself within the institution's special environment for learning. Thus he claims that independent study should be self-pacing, individualized, and offer freedom in goal selection.

The independent learner

Wedemeyer sees the independent learner as the original or 'proto'-learner whose success in learning enables him to survive and he claims that each individual commences with a period of pre-school individual learning. Group instruction which evolved in schools was first intended, he tells us, for the elite, and the long history of formal education is characterized by a persistent pattern of the learner in the group - a *dependent* learner whose goals, activities, rewards, and punishments are decided by the policies and practices of an ever-present group of teachers.

The pattern of the learner in the group underwent a gradual breakdown process in which he sees the space and time barriers to independent study being dissipated in six successive stages:

1. The invention of writing.
2. The invention of printing.
3. The invention of correspondence education: the first formally structured format for the independent learner, which made use of new technology in the form of a reliable mail service in the mid-1800s.
4. Development of democratic and egalitarian philosophies.
5. Application of telecommunications media to teaching.
6. Development of programmed-learning theory.

(Wedemeyer 1973:75)

These series of developments led in his own day to the possibility for people, cut off from the regular schools, to continue learning in ever larger numbers. Wedemeyer uses three terms for such programmes: 'independent study', 'open learning', and 'distance education'. He saw in the 1960s the re-emergence of the independent learner, with a new elan for independent programmes in areas where conventional group-based formal learning was less able to succeed.

'Independent study'

Wedemeyer made a determined effort to establish the term 'independent study' as the umbrella term for this field of education both in the US and throughout the world:

> Independent study consists of various forms of teaching-learning arrangements in which teachers and learners carry out their essential tasks and responsibilities apart from one another, communicating in a variety of ways. Its purposes are to free on-campus or internal learners from inappropriate class placings or patterns, to provide off-campus or external learners with the opportunity to continue learning in their own environments, and developing in all learners the capacity to carry on self-directed learning, the ultimate maturity required of the educated person.
>
> (Wedemeyer 1977:2114)

It will be noticed at once that Wedemeyer's concept of 'independent study' comprises two different forms of education: 'independent study for the internal student' and 'independent study for the external student'. Independent study for the internal student makes freedom from lecture attendance possible for exceptional university students by the allocation of series of readings and individual study programmes. One can see elements in his thought of ideas similar to the contract programmes and educational brokerage ideas favoured in some experimental American programmes of the mid-1970s. The linking of external and internal programmes in the one definition, however, tends to diffuse Wedemeyer's ideas and the emphasis on internal independent study disappears in his later articles.

Wedemeyer's liberal educational theory and egalitarian social philosophy were ill-at-ease with the conventional educational system and many of his writings are marked by comments on the shortcomings of the contemporary scene both at school and university level:

> Conventional teaching and learning, makes use of concepts of learning and teaching that have preserved the old mystiques, that have maintained space-time barriers to learning.
>
> (Childs and Wedemeyer 1961:71)

Within this context he set out a conceptual structure for an educational system that would be more akin to his views. Most of his writings list ten characteristics of the proposed system:

1. The system should be capable of operation any place where there are students - or even only one student - whether or not there are teachers at the same place at the same time.
2. The system should place greater responsibility for learning on the student.
3. The system should free faculty members from custodial type duties so that more time can be given to truly educational tasks.
4. The system should offer students and adults wider choices (more opportunities) in courses, formats, methodologies.
5. The system should use, as appropriate, all the teaching media and methods that have been proved effective.
6. The system should mix and combine media and methods so that each subject or unit within a subject is taught in the best way known.
7. The system should cause the redesign and development of courses to fit into an 'articulated media programme'.
8. The system should preserve and enhance opportunities for adaptation to individual differences.
9. The system should evaluate student achievement simply, not by raising barriers concerned *with the place* the student studies, the *rate* at which he studies, the *method* by which he studies or the *sequence* within which he studies.
10. The system should permit students to start, stop and learn at their own pace.

(Wedemeyer 1968:328, 1981:36)

Wedemeyer saw instinctively that the only way to break what he called the 'space-time barriers' of education was by separating teaching from learning. This involved planning each as a separate activity. These early insights by Wedemeyer were later confirmed by Kaye and Rumble (1978).

Planning teaching and learning as separate activities leads Wedemeyer to postulate six characteristics of distance or independent systems that are capable of operation any place there are students - or even only one student - whether or not there are teachers at the same place at the same time:

1. The student and teacher are separated.
2. The normal processes of teaching and learning are

carried on in writing or through some other medium.
3. Teaching is individualized.
4. Learning takes place through the student's activity.
5. Learning is made convenient for the student in his own environment.
6. The learner takes responsibility for his progress, with freedom to start and stop at any time and to pace himself.

(Wedemeyer 1973:76)

The teaching-learning situation

In many of his writings Wedemeyer presents his thoughts diagramatically. He claims that every teaching-learning situation comprises four elements:

a teacher
a learner or learners
a communications system or mode
something to be taught/learned.

He then claims that a traditional classroom could be represented as a box which encompasses the four elements as shown in Fig. 4.1.

Figure 4.1 The classroom as a teaching-learning situation (Wedemeyer)

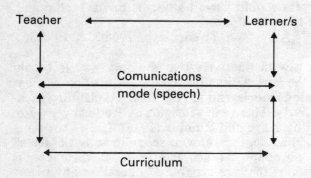

Source: Adapted from Keegan (ed.) 1976

58

In a number of his writings Wedemeyer explains what he has called the 'classroom-box':

If the communications system is a given, either because it is the only system available (think of Plato meeting learners in the Grove of Akademos) or is a cultural artifact acting as an imperative, then there are no options, and the communication must be face-to-face, eyeball-to-eyeball, earpan-to-earpan speech. Then, if a box is put around the four essential elements, we have a classroom. A teaching-learning system that must work any place, any time, for one learner or many, directly confronts the space-time-elite barriers of the classroom model. In fact, however, distance has long been a problem in the classroom model. As classes became larger, and lectures replaced the dialogue that Plato conducted, the integrity of the model was breached. Only the illusion of being effectively face-to-face remains, as distance within the box lengthens between teacher and learners and speech is amplified for ever more distant reception. The concept of 'distance' involves more than physical distance. There is social distance, cultural distance, and what I have been calling 'physical' distance for want of a better term. All of these are present wherever teaching and learning are carried on.
(Wedemeyer 1981:38–40, 1978:13–14)

However if we are to achieve a 'teaching-learning system that can work any place, any time, for one learner or many', Wedemeyer tells us that the 'classroom-box' (Fig. 4.1) must be restructured as in Fig. 4.2.

Figure 4.2 A teaching-learning situation to accommodate physical distance (Wedemeyer)

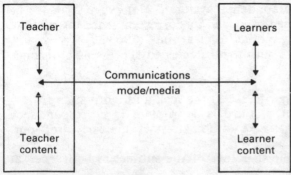

Source: Adapted from Keegan (ed.) 1976

The four elements of the previous structure remain but have been reorganized to accommodate physical space.This representation of the teaching-learning process by Wedemeyer to accommodate the 'any time, any place, single or multiple learner's requirements' has as its aim the organization of instruction so that greater freedom in learning is possible. As an outcome of this he proposes three conceptualizations of freedom for learners in all independent or distance programmes:

- learning should be self-pacing: the learner should be able to pace his studies in accordance with his circumstances and needs
- learning should be individualized and the learners should be free to follow any of several courses of learning
- the learner should have freedom in selection of goals and activities.

(Wedemeyer 1973:101)

Structuring the system

Wedemeyer ran into some criticism when he tried to suggest that these theoretical propositions about the freedom of the distance learner should be implemented in practice. These criticisms came both from those looking for a workable system and from those who feared that public monies spent on distance systems would be transferred back to conventional education if the learning in the distance system could not be accurately evaluated or if the evaluation was that the learning in the independent system was inferior.

Despite the idealistic nature of much of Wedemeyer's writing he had a very extensive knowledge of the day-to-day workings of correspondence systems. 'Not every student', he warns, 'will be able to succeed by correspondence instruction. This is *not* an easy method of learning' (1963:30).

He details five serious obstacles to success as a distance learner:

- developing interest in the task and motivation
- readiness for study is a problem in correspondence study witnessed by 'the non-start, the early drop-out, the under achiever'
- grasping the structure of the subject to be learned at a distance
- learning both analytic and instructive thinking

• evaluating progress in learning.

(Wedemeyer 1962:14)

The secret of success in Wedemeyer's thought is placed squarely on the shoulders of the instructor who is in a continuous tutorial relationship with the correspondence student. The teacher is the daily monitor and motivator of the distance student. The chief value of the correspondence method lies in the tutorial relationship developed between the teacher and the student, and to minimize or destroy this relationship (by check-off type lessons, multiple-choice answers) actually changes the character of the work offered. Schools that depend solely on the use of objective or machine-type scoring have abandoned distance education. Such programmes are, in fact, programmes of 'self-study' (1963:29).

In a similar vein Wedemeyer does not consider close-circuit television, radio, telephone, teaching machines, computer, and satellite as forms of independent study or distance education except under strict conditions: 'If media (CCTV, for example) are employed merely to replicate a regular class without broadening opportunity and shifting responsibility and freedom to the learner, the system cannot be defined as independent study' (1971:552).

Evaluation

Wedemeyer undertook the uphill struggle of trying to promote non-traditional education programmes in the highly structured US university scene. The rather bleak title he chose for the edited collection of his writings published on his retirement, *Learning at the Back-Door*, shows his own assessment of the Sisyphan task of gaining status for non-traditional, open, and distance programmes for credit in the US.

Wedemeyer's earlier writings are more incisive than his later articles which tend to reproduce with precision ideas presented earlier. All the important ideas are there in the 1960s and there is little reformulation in the 1970s. Although the writings of the 1960s show familiarity with the day-to-day problems of the organization of independent programmes and the difficulties of both teaching and learning at a distance, he does not deal with planning mechanisms or management analyses that would allow others to build on his ideas.

Ellis claimed that Wedemeyer's criteria for conducting a distance education system 'lacked specific context, purposes, constraints and cost-consciousness' (1978:16-17).

The criticism of conventional schooling and university education in Wedemeyer's writings is frequent. Progress for distance education does not lie down this cul-de-sac. Criticism of on-campus programmes calls for the improvement of on-campus programmes, not for the development of distance systems.

The difficult status of American distance education in the 1970s and early 1980s shows the necessity for more thinkers like Wedemeyer to focus on the specific context of university education in the United States of America. His personal dedication, generosity, and liberal vision contributed much to the growth of a consensus among distance educators throughout the world and influenced many of the writers treated in the next chapters.

AUTONOMY AND DISTANCE

Writing in 1973, Michael G. Moore, formerly of the University of Wisconsin at Madison, then of the Open University of the United Kingdom and today at Pennsylvania State University, complained that progress in distance education was being hindered by lack of attention to what he called the 'macro-factors':

• description
• definition
• discrimination
• identification
• building a theoretical framework.

His own contribution was the development of a theory of distance education based on the variables 'autonomy' and 'distance'.

Moore's first contributions to a theory of distance education came in the early 1970s but they read with surprising freshness today. A number of themes are immediately apparent in his writing: he states clearly that he wishes to develop a theory of education at a distance, defines which aspects of educational endeavour he is dealing with and which are excluded, speaks of those students who *will* not attend groupings but choose to learn apart from teachers, uses confidently terms like 'distance teaching' and 'distance education' as 'a field of education' at a time when most were classifying it merely as a method or a mode (Moore 1975). Moore's focus is on all forms of deliberate, planned, structured learning and teaching that are carried on outside the school environment. He defines the school environment as 'the classroom, lecture or seminar, the setting in which the events of teaching are contemporaneous and co-terminous with the events of learning'. Distance education (he uses the term 'independent learning and teaching') is an educational system in which the learner is autonomous and separated from the teacher by space and time so that communication is by a non-human medium. The distance system has three subsystems: a learner, a teacher and a method of communication. These subsystems have critical characteristics distinguishing them from learning, teaching, and communication in other forms of education.

His research began with the belief that instruction can be considered as comprising two families of teaching activities: face-to-face or 'contiguous' teaching and 'distance teaching'. From an exhaustive search of the literature, Moore lists the forms of educational provision that fall within his concept of 'distance teaching': an open university, a university without walls, an independent study programme on-campus, an external degree programme, and even a teach-yourself book. This is a much wider classification than that accepted for distance education in this book. The reason for it is, as with Wedemeyer, the inclusion of on-campus independent study programmes within the definition, and an opening up of the concept 'independence' to include programmes without two-way communication.

Within this theoretical structure Moore identifies two clusters of educational offerings as essential components of independent study:

- programmes designed for learners in environments apart from their instructors - distance teaching; and
- programmes designed for the encouragement of indepen-dent/self-directed learning - learner autonomy.

Here he brings together two traditions: distance teaching which he traces back (with Noffsinger) to the 1840s and self-directed study which he traces back through a range of practices in American higher education to the tutor system in Oxford University in the nineteenth century.

Distance teaching is defined as the family of instructional methods in which the teaching behaviours are executed apart from the learning behaviours, including those behaviours that in a contiguous situation would be performed in the learner's presence, so that communication between the teacher and the learner must be facilitated by print, electronic, mechanical, or other devices (1977a:68).

Moore accepted that teaching consists of two phases: 'the preactive' and the 'interactive'. For Moore, the teacher in the preactive phase selects objectives and plans the curriculum and instructional strategies. In the 'interactive' phase, face-to-face with learners, the teacher provides verbal stimulation, makes explanations, asks questions, and provides guidance (1977b:15).

He is clearly concerned that most educational research treats teaching as 'the activity which takes place *during* school and *within* the classroom setting' where communication is by the human voice and there is 'immediate, spontaneous, often emotionally-motivated interaction between the learner and the teacher, and usually between the learner and other learners: there is a social interactional relationship which assumes no delay in communication, no distance in space or time'. Since the introduction of compulsory education for children, Moore points out, face-to-face teaching has been accepted as the norm. But distance teaching situations do exist, particularly with adult learners.

The concept of distance

Moore correctly identifies the concept of separation of learner and teacher as the origin of the concept 'distance' in education, and as crucial for determining the selection of research data from which theoretical frameworks in this field may be constructed. Basic to Moore's position is that distance teaching programmes can be classified according to the distance between learner and teacher. He wants programmes to be classified by the provision for two-way communication (dialogue or D) and by the extent to which a programme can be responsive to a learner's individual needs (structure or S). He believes that the element of two-way communication in all distance teaching programmes can be measured and suggests that an educational telephone network is an example of high two-way communication or dialogue (+D) and an educational radio broadcast is an example of a distance teaching methodology in which two-way communication is *not* possible (-D) and hence would not be counted as an example of distance education as defined in this book. (He is classifying educational uses of media, not communications media.)

Moore also measures programmes in so far as they are responsive to students' needs as individuals, and labels this 'structure'. In a highly structured programme (+S) no variation of the programme is possible (as in a Linear Programmed Instruction Text), but when there is a minimum of structure teachers and learners can respond easily to stimuli. Thus Moore feels it is important to measure the extent of the responsiveness of a teaching programme to a learner's individual needs, goals, progress, or achievements (is it highly structured or not?) whether the communications medium on which it is based permits two-way communication or not. He presents this as in Table 4.1 (with S representing structure and D dialogue).

Table 4.1 Types of distance teaching programmes (Moore)

	Type	*Programme types*	*Examples*
Most distance	-D-S	1. Programmes with no dialogue and no structure	Independent reading-study programmes of the 'self-directed' kind
	-D+S	2. Programmes with no dialogue but with structure	Programmes in which the communication method is radio or television
	+D+S	3. Programmes with dialogue and structure	Typically programmes using the correspondence method
Least distance	+D-S	4. Programmes with dialogue and no structure	A Rogerian type of tutorial programme

Source: Adapted from Moore (1977a).

The concept of autonomy

The more tentative section of Moore's theory is when he tries to establish learner autonomy as the second dimension of independent learning (1972).

In his various publications Moore writes well on the autonomy of the independent learner. There is a strong humanistic tendency in his writing. He is influenced by Charles Wedemeyer, Carl Rogers, Allan Tough, and Malcolm Knowles, but the synthesis is his own. Starting from a general observation that learners both in schools and universities are very dependent on teachers for explanations, guidance, questions, and stimulation, Moore shows that such an approach places more decision-making powers in the hands of the teacher than is acceptable to some adult education theorists.

Like Wedemeyer he seeks for learner autonomy in:

- the setting of objectives
- methods of study
- evaluation.

There *are* possible programmes, he tells us, that achieve these goals but most do not. Both in conventional education and in most programmes of distance teaching and learning, Moore supports Maslow's analysis that the teacher is the active one who teaches a passive person. This person is shaped and taught and is given something which he then accumulates and which he may lose or retain. This kind of learning, he tells us, too easily reflects the goals of the teacher, and ignores the values and ends of the learner (1977b:21).

The basis for learner autonomy as a necessary theoretical component of distance education is justified by Moore from his analysis of the separation between teacher and learner in education at a distance. He asks whether the concept of 'distance' or 'separation' or 'apartness' is adequate to explain the gap between teacher and learner. His own answer is no. The existence of this gap means that the activities of teachers and learners will be influenced by it. Because the learner *is* alone, he is compelled to accept a comparatively high degree of responsibility for the conduct of the learning programme. The learner also exercises a greater degree of control over his/her learning.

The autonomous learner proceeds without need for admonition and little need for direction. If highly autonomous he may have no personal relationship with a teacher but if he *has* a personal teacher he will be able to control the effect and significance of teacher input in a realistic and unemotional way. To the highly autonomous learner the teacher's role is that of respondent rather than director and the institution becomes a helping organization.

There are some adult learners who need help in formulating their learning objectives and in identifying sources of information and in measuring achievements, whereas there are many others who are autonomous learners, with the abilities of self-stimulation, knowledge of ways to achieve their objectives, and ways of measuring achievement. It is necessary, therefore, to be able to measure the 'autonomy' dimension of educational programmes. Moore sets out to do this in terms of his statement that all teaching-learning processes have these characteristic components:

- *establishment or preparatory activities* in which problems are identified, goals set and strategies planned
- *executive activities* in which data, information and ideas are patterned, experiments and tests take place in order to arrive at instructional solutions
- *evaluatory activities* in which the instructional processes make judgements about the appropriateness of the information and ideas for solving the problems and meeting the goals.

(Moore 1977b:21)

Moore claims that in conventional education the establishment activities are entirely in the purview of the teacher, whereas at a distance the teacher merely prepares instructional materials to be used and drawn upon to the extent that the learner desires. The teacher hopes that his material will meet the goals established by learners and will be used in their executive activities. In distance education, whether or not the material is used remains outside the distant teacher's control, and is dependent almost entirely on the worth of the material, as distant learners accept only executive material that meets their goals.

Similarly in evaluation, the conventional teacher invariably establishes both the criteria of successful learning and passes judgement on whether the criteria are satisfied. Where the teachers' and learners' goals do not coincide the latter invariably compromise through fear, apathy, or courtesy. Learner autonomy is heightened by distance and the learner is compelled by distance to assume a degree of autonomy that might be uncomfortable in other circumstances.

Classification of programmes

Programmes are classified according to the extent to which the learner can exercise autonomy in learning by asking three questions:

- *Autonomy in setting of objectives?* Is the selection of learning objectives in the programme that of the learner or the teacher?
- *Autonomy in methods of study?* Is the selection and use of

resource persons, of bodies, and other media, the decision of the teacher or the learner?

- *Autonomy in evaluation?* Are the decisions about the method of evaluation and criteria to be used made by the learner or the teacher?

By applying these questions to teaching programmes Moore arrives at the classification shown in Table 4.2 in which A = learner determined (autonomous) and N = teacher determined (non-autonomous). An indication of the type of programme Moore might be considering is given for each of his eight categories.

Table 4.2 Types of independent study programmes by variable of learner autonomy (Moore)

Example	*Objective setting*	*Implemen- tation*	*Evaluat- ion*
1. Private study	A	A	A
2. University of London External Degree	A	A	N
3. Learning sports skills	A	N	A
4. Learning car driving	A	N	N
5. Learner controls course and evaluation	N	A	A
6. Learner controls evaluation	N	N	A
7. Many independent study courses	N	A	N
8. Independent study for credit	N	N	N

A = Learner determined ('autonomous').
N = Teacher determined ('non-autonomous').

Source: Adapted from Moore (1977a).

Since learner autonomy is the extent to which in an independent study programme the learner determines the objectives, implementation strategies and evaluation and since distance means a combination of the availability of two-way communication plus the extent to which a programme is adaptable to the individuality of students, it follows that Moore can classify all educational programmes by his own variables 'distance' and 'autonomy'. This he proposes to do by superimposing Table 4.1 on Table 4.2 in such a way that he can categorize all educational programmes so that they range from having most independent to the least independent study.

In Fig. 4.3 type AAA-D-S represents the most independent form of education: totally private study with no two-way communication and completely unstructured with the learner entirely autonomous in goals, methods, and evaluation. Type NNN+D-S is the least independent, where autonomy and distance are very low and the learner is completely controlled by the teacher.

Figure 4.3 Typology of educational programmes (Moore)

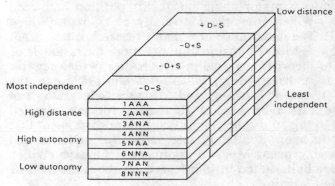

Source: Adapted from Moore (1977a)

Thus, for Moore, independent study is any educational programme in which the learning programme occurs separate in time and place from the teaching programme, and in which the learner has an influence equal to the teacher's in determining learning goals, resources, and evaluation decisions.

But learners vary in the extent to which they are able to exercise autonomy and hence there is no value judgement in the use of the terms 'autonomy' and 'distance'. There are programmes with much autonomy and dialogue and programmes with less, and they vary in distance. A programme of high autonomy may be as damaging to a person as one of low autonomy. The problem is to match programmes to learners so that each learner exercises the maximum autonomy and grows.

Evaluation

The first pole of his theoretical position 'distance' is well established, but further contribution is required from Moore to justify 'autonomy' (1972, 1983) as a second pole.

Moore recommenced publication on distance education after transferring from the Open University of the UK to Pennsylvania State University. A monograph *Self-directed Learning and Distance Education* (Moore 1983) restated his positions of the 1970s.

A major *Epistolodidaktika* article (Moore 1985) followed, in which he reviewed research on distance education since his major contributions a decade earlier. He judged that some progress had, in fact, been made but that the discipline of distance education had reached the stage in 1985 that the discipline of adult education had reached 20 to 30 years previously.

Meanwhile a major challenge to his position had been mounted by Willén from the University of Uppsala (Willén 1981, 1983). The importance of Willén's research is that it not only challenges Moore's position but questions the rationale of the group of theorists analysed in this chapter. Willén's major analysis was published in *Epistolodidaktika* in 1987 under the title 'Self-directed learning and distance education: can distance education be a good alternative for self-directed learners?'. In this study she claims that Moore's statement that distance education is a good alternative for self-directed learners is unproven. Moore's arguments, she says (Willén 1987:52), are built on too little information about the facts of self-directed learning.

In 1988 in an article published in *Distance Education*, Willén took up a position even further apart from Moore:

> (In) Moore's theory of 'independent learning and teaching' ... the pupil is regarded as a person willing and able to work through an educational programme on his own, these personal qualities being his foremost reasons for enrolling for this type of teaching. The foundation of the theory, i.e. that distance students choose this kind of teaching because they have special personal qualities is not corroborated by surveys. Distance teaching is chosen mainly for practical reasons.
>
> (Willén 1988:77)

Willén poses a fundamental challenge not only to all the writers in this group but to all who see distance education as characterized by independence and autonomy. She is claiming that her research shows that ideas of independence and autonomy are not borne out by reality. Distance students, she says, have much the same characteristics as other adult students and the same needs.

Despite some recent contributions (Moore 1988) Moore does not seem to have recognized the seriousness of Willén's challenge. His new position as professor at Pennsylvania State University with special responsibility for distance education may enable him to re-enter this crucial area of distance education research.

REFERENCES

Childs, G. and Wedemeyer, C.A. (1961) *New Perspectives in University Correspondence Study*, Chicago: Centre for Study of Education of Adults.

Delling, R.M. (1966) 'Versuch der Grundlegung zu einer systematischen Theorie des Fernunterrichts', in L. Sroka (ed.) *Fernunterricht 1966, Festschrift zum 50 Geburtstag von Walter Schultz-Rahe*. Hamburg: Hamburger Fernlehristitut.

Delling, R.M. (1968) 'Protokoll des I Brief-Symposions über Fernunterrich und Fernstudium', *Epistoldidaktika* 1 (Sonderheft), 6-10.

Delling, R.M. (1978) 'Briefwechsel als Bestandteil und Vorlaufer des Fernstudiums' (*Ziff Papiere 19*), Hagen: Fernuniversität (ZIFF).

Ellis, J. (1978) 'A response to Charles A. Wedemeyer', *Canadian Journal of University Continuing Education* 6(1), 16-17.

Holmberg, B. (1960) *On the Methods of Teaching by Correspondence*, Lund: Gleerup.

Kaye, A. and Rumble, G. (1978) *Distance Teaching for Higher and Adult Education*, London: Croom Helm.

Keegan, D. (ed.) (1976) *TAFE Distance Education in South Australia*, Adelaide: Open College.

Moore, M. (1972) 'Learner autonomy: the second dimension of independent learning', *Convergence* 5(2), 76-8.

Moore, M. (1973) 'Toward a theory of independent learning and teaching', *Journal of Higher Education* 44, 661-79.

Moore, M. (1975) 'Cognitive style and telemathic (distance) teaching', *ICCE Newsletter* 4, 3-10.

Moore, M. (1977a) 'A model of independent study',

Epistolodidaktika 1, 6-40.

Moore, M. (1977b) *On a Theory of Independent Study*, Hagen: Fernuniversität.

Moore, M. (1983) 'The individual adult learner', in M. Tight (ed.) *Adult Learning and Education* London: Croom Helm.

Moore, M. (1985) 'Some observations on current research in distance education', *Epistolodidaktika* 1, 35-62.

Moore, M. (1988) 'Telecommunications, internationalism and distance education', *American Journal of Distance Education* 2(1), 1-7.

Reichert, J. (1959) *Schreiben, Lehren und Verstehen*, Freiburg: Bergakademie.

Wedemeyer, C. (1962) Report of the Conference on Newer Media in Correspondence Study, Austin, Texas: University Texas, pp.10-14.

Wedemeyer, C. (1963) 'Going to college at home', *Home Study Review* 4(3), 24-32.

Wedemeyer, C. (1968) 'With whom will you dance? The new educational technology', *Journal of the American Dietetic Association* 53, 325-8.

Wedemeyer, C. (1971) 'Independent study', in L. Deighton (ed.) *The Encyclopedia of Education*, New York: Macmillan, vol. 4, pp. 548-57.

Wedemeyer, C. (1973) 'The use of correspondence education for post-secondary education', in A. Kabwasa and M. Kaunda (eds) *Correspondence Education in Africa*, London: Routledge & Kegan Paul.

Wedemeyer, C. (1974) 'Characteristics of open learning systems', in *Open Learning Systems*, Washington: National Association of Educational Broadcasters.

Wedemeyer, C. (1977) 'Independent study', in A.S. Knowles (ed.) *The International Encyclopedia of Higher Education*, Boston: CIHED, pp. 2114-32.

Wedemeyer, C. (1978) 'Criteria for constructing and distance education system', *Canadian Journal of University Continuing Education* 6(1), 9-15.

Wedemeyer, C. (1981) *Learning at the Back-Door*, Madison: University of Wisconsin.

Willén, B. (1981) *Distance Education at Swedish Universities*, Uppsala: Almqvist & Wiksell.

Willén, B. (1983) Distance Education in Swedish Universities, *Distance Education* 4(2), 211-22.

Willén, B. (1987) 'Self-directed learning and distance education', *Epistolodidaktika*, 2, 52-69.

Willén, B. (1988) 'What happened to the Open University - in brief', *Distance Education* 9(1), 71-83.

Chapter Five

THE INDUSTRIALIZATION OF TEACHING

Anyone professionally involved in education is obliged to presume the existence of two forms of instruction which are strictly separable: traditional face-to-face teaching based on interpersonal communication and industrialised teaching which is based on an objectivised, rationalised, technologically-produced interaction.

O. Peters 1973

INTRODUCTION

Much of the early research work in distance education was accomplished by Otto Peters in the early 1960s. Peters worked at the German Institute for Distance Education (DIFF) at Tübingen in the Federal Republic of Germany, then at the Berlin College of Education before becoming in 1975 the foundation Vice-Chancellor (*Gründungsrektor*) of the Fernuniversität in Hagen. In 1965 he published an authoritative analytical and comparative survey of distance institutions at further educational level throughout the world. This was followed in 1968 by a survey of distance teaching at higher education level.

Peters states that when his analytical and comparative analysis of distance teaching systems was complete, he proceeded to develop a theoretical structure for the field. He claims that the traditional categories of educational research proved inadequate for a didactical analysis of distance systems and he was forced to abandon them. Building up systems for teaching at a distance, he tells us, is structured so differently from conventional, oral education that the didactical analyst must look elsewhere for his models.

For Peters the most fruitful model was the similarities between the industrial production process and the teaching/

learning process in distance education. He analysed the industrial production process and found that not only did this provide a satisfactory basis for an analysis of distance teaching but that a fruitful explanatory and forecasting theory of teaching at a distance was possible when one considered it as the most industrialized form of teaching and learning.

Peters justified his search for a new theoretical basis for distance teaching on the grounds that it is a new form of industrialized and technological education. He states that from many points of view conventional, oral, group-based education is a pre-industrial form of education. In the universities of the Middle Ages, the ancient rhetorical form of education was replaced by the lecture, the seminar, and the lesson and these have remained permanent characteristics of traditional education ever since. The humanistic influence added the tutorial. These can all be regarded as pre-industrialized forms of education in which the individual lecturer remains in close contact with the whole teaching process just as an artisan does with his craft. Attempts to adapt the lecture, seminar, and tutorial to industrialized techniques by the use of educational technology will not prove successful because of the pre-industrial characteristics of the didactic structures in conventional universities.

Distance teaching, however, is recent. It could not have existed before the Industrial Era. It began, at most, 130 years ago, he says, writing in 1980. It was no historical accident that correspondence education and the industrialization of society began about the same time because they are intrinsically linked. Distance education is impossible without a relatively fast and regular postal service and transport system: 'the first railway lines and the first correspondence schools were established around the same time'.

Traditional educational concepts are only of partial use in analysing and describing this industrialized form of education so new categories for analysis must be found and they can best be found from the sciences which analyse industrial processes.

All forms of human life have been heavily influenced by the industrial revolution. Only traditional forms of education in schools, colleges, and universities have remained outside it - except for the phenomenon of education at a distance.

Peters claims some basis for his comparative study from the fact that the production of learning materials for distance students is, in itself, an industrialized process and one that is, in its didactic procedures, quite different from book production.

DIDACTICAL ANALYSIS

Peters' theoretical presentation of distance teaching commences with a didactical analysis. In this presentation distance teaching is analysed as a distinct field of educational endeavour and not as a teaching 'mode'. The analysis of the didactic structure of distance teaching (1967:3-17) follows exactly the structures proposed by Paul Heimann and Wolfgang Schultz, two German educational technologists who founded the Berlin School of Didactics - now also referred to as the Hamburg model, as Schultz became a professor at the University of Hamburg (Heidt 1978:48; Holmberg 1982:139).

Heimann and Schultz claim that all teaching-learning processes can be analysed in terms of six intrinsic structural elements: aims, content, methods, choice of medium, human pre-requisites, and socio-cultural pre-requisites. Peters analyses distance education, as Heimann and Schultz had analysed education in general, in terms of these six essential structures of the educational process and has little difficulty in demonstrating profound structural differences between distance education and conventional education for all six of the constituent characteristics (1967:4-16).

- *Aim*: The aim of distance teaching is determined by structural considerations as in all forms of teaching. Specific structural differences in the cognitive, emotional, and practical domains are indicated for distance teaching.
- *Contents*: The teaching of knowledge, skills, and practical 'hand-on' learning are examined and the difficulties and/or possibility of teaching certain content at a distance is considered.
- *Methods*: The drastic reduction or complete suppression of interpersonal communication is treated and its substitution by written information carriers and motivators.
- *Choice of medium*: It is claimed that communication suffers an essential loss of substance in its transfer from human speech to the written word and the possible compensating role of other media is considered.
- *Human pre-requisites*: Employment conditions, age, diagnostic counselling for entry to courses are contrasted with the condition of conventional students.
- *Socio-cultural pre-requisites*: Ideological, political, academic status, and tradition aspects of distance education in different cultures (USA, USSR, South Africa, England, Sweden) are considered.

The conclusion for Peters is inescapable. Distance education and conventional education have been shown to be essentially diverse on each of the six constituent components of an educational process as defined by the most 'adequate theoretical basis for dealing with instructional media' (Heidt 1978:47) known to German educational theorists.

This analysis leads to a fundamental separation between direct and indirect teaching and the claim that educational theorists have focused on direct teaching, especially in its conventional, oral, group-based form to the virtual exclusion of that other component of the educational scene - indirect teaching - of which distance teaching is one of the elements.

He lists the other components of teaching which are not direct, but which are not, however, to be identified as distance education: education by letter; printed learning materials; audio-visual teaching; educational radio and television; programmed learning; computer-based instruction; independent study; private study; and learning from teaching materials.

INDUSTRIAL COMPARISON

At this point in his treatment of the subject (1967, 1971, 1973, 1981) Peters presents a comparison of distance teaching and the industrial production of goods under the following headings: rationalization; division of labour; mechanization; assembly line; mass production; preparatory work; formalization; standardization; functional change; objectification; concentration; and centralization.

- *Rationalization* is seen as a characteristic of distance teaching when the knowledge and skills of a teacher are transmitted to a theoretically unlimited number of students by the detached objectivity of a distance education course of constant quality.
- *Division of labour* is the main pre-requisite for the advantages of distance teaching to become effective and is thus a constituent element of it. If the number of students enroled in a distance course is high, regular assessment of performance is not carried out by those academics who developed the course and other elements of the teaching/learning process are assigned to others.
- *Mechanization*. Conventional education proceeds at a pre-industrial level with the teacher using the tools of the trade (pictures, objects, books) without these changing the

structure of teaching; in distance teaching mechanization eventually changes the nature of the teaching process.

- *Assembly line.* In distance teaching the staff remain at their posts but the teaching (manuscript for example) is passed from one area of responsibility to another and specific changes are made at each stage.
- *Mass production.* Traditional forms of teaching envisage small groups and can only be applied to mass education artificially (e.g. a loudspeaker from one lecture hall to an adjoining one). Distance teaching copes confidently with mass production which is essential to it.
- *Planning and preparation.* As in industry, distance teaching is characterized by extensive planning by senior specialist staff in special departments and prior financial investment. Success is linked to the preparatory phase in a way that is different from conventional teaching.
- *Standardization.* A greater degree of standardization is required than in conventional teaching and the educational advantages of the interesting deviation at a particular time with a particular group of students is not possible: the objective requirements of the total course profile dominate the particular interests of the teacher.
- *Functional change and objectification* are further essential elements of the most industrialized form of education, especially when the functional role of teacher is split at least three ways: provider of knowledge (distance unit author), evaluator of knowledge and progress (course maker or tutor), and counsellor (subject programme adviser).
- *Monopolization.* Concentration and centralization are characteristics of the management of distance systems and of industrial enterprise; distance teaching institutions have a tendency to monopolization within a state or national educational provision.

EDUCATIONAL TECHNOLOGY

The completion of this comparative study of distance education and the industrial production of goods led Peters to an analysis of distance teaching in the light of the then current ideas (mid-1960s) about educational technology. He follows distance education through five groupings of educational technologists which he takes over from the German didactician Flechsig:

Theories of distance education

1. simulation models,
2. planning models (*Zweckrationalität*),
3. materials development strategies,
4. systems approach,
5. curriculum development.

Peters studies the affinities between distance education and educational technology, especially programmed learning. He shares with Flechsig and the educational technologists of the period the belief that planning and technology will achieve educational success. It was felt that the application of technical categories to educational processes would achieve beneficial results and that systematic planning and rationalization of educational means to reach defined goals (*Zweckrationalität*) could achieve both educational and economic efficiency.

CONCLUSIONS

The final dimension of Peter's analysis of distance education is what he calls the historical, sociological and anthropological perspective. Humanistic attacks on the industrialization of society and its contribution to mass culture lead Peters to expect criticism from humanists of his theory of distance education as the most industrialized form of education.

Tracing the historical evolution of educational structures back to early Indo-European origins, Peters finds them characterized by six elements:

- elitism
- sacral aspects
- hierarchical aspects
- family-small group structures
- personal communication
- time-place-person ties.

Distance education is the final phase of the evolution of education away from these sociological structures. It presents a new, strange, and foreign educational pattern that also has six characteristics, being

- egalitarian
- profane
- democratic
- aimed at a mass audience
- technologically-based

• free from the dimensions of educational time, places and persons.

A sociological analysis based on the German philosophical *Gemeinschaft/Gesellschaft* positions taken from Weber, Tönnies, and Habermas shows that traditional, oral, group-based education follows the *'Gemeinschaft'* categorization with distance education falling into the *'Gesellschaft'* grouping. In general terms *'Gemeinschaft'* structures are friendly and community-based; *Gesellschaft* implies a wider, society-based structure that may be unfriendly. The communication processes within these two sociological groupings show that the intersubjectivity and reciprocity of interpersonal communication in conventional education is radically to be contrasted with the 'context-free', mechanical communication of education at a distance. The possibility of alienation is not overlooked.

Peters sees as practical consequences of his theory that there is something unnatural about education at a distance. The process of communication is broken up and artificial substitutes for it are provided. The whole communication process is changed and this changes the teaching acts and the learning acts which take place in the education system.

Peters feels that it is a slow process for a teacher to adapt to a distance education system because there will always be clashes between traditional teaching and the carefully structured procedures of a distance teaching university, in which the unity of the teaching/learning process is split into many units performed by different persons and elements of the education system. The process of adaptation however can be furthered by reflection on the characteristics of distance education.

The student in an industrialized education system finds that instruction is available in such ways that he can choose his own way. Instruction is not linked to fixed times, to fixed places, to fixed persons. This throws new responsibilities on the learner that are not characteristic of pre-industrialized education systems.

Peters has no desire to criticize conventional education. His view, however, is that industrialized society of today has developed so many needs for education that it is absurd to imagine that conventional systems can satisfy them. New techniques are needed and these must be industrial.

He recognizes that traditionalists will say: What happens to the highly valued traditions of face-to-face education? What happens to the spirit of the learning community? These are all, he admits, of value but you cannot have 40,000-50,000 students in a system like an open university and try to provide face-to-face tuition with finite means.

Almost alone among distance educators writing about distance education, Peters finds much to query in the industrialization of education. He finds distance education unnatural; it breaks up the process of communication; artificial mechanical substitutes for interpersonal communication are provided; this changes the teaching behaviours and the learning behaviours; there is a definite propensity to alienation. If you are going to teach in the most industrialized form of education, he tells us, you have to be ready to live with the problems that the industrialization of education brings.

EVALUATION

Reactions and objections to Peters' thesis have been many and there are those who deplore the introduction of industrial concepts into an educational field. Four of these reactions are considered here: Christof Ehmann, Karl-Heinz Rebel, Manfred Hamann, and integrationist responses.

Christof Ehmann

Ehmann (1981:231) criticizes Peters' position because of its dependence on faith in the value of planning in education and faith in technical progress. He claims that these faiths, strong in the 1960s, have been shown to be wrong in the 1980s and that 'the application of technical categories to social processes is just as questionable as the use of biological analogies'. Planning euphoria, programmed learning, faith in the calculability of processes - all central features of Peters' industrialized models - have all been dissipated before the 1980s started.

Ehmann's evaluation of Peter's contribution is negative. He feels that as an academic position it is largely dated because of its reliance on theories of planning and technical progress, that its influence on Peters' own institution - the Fernuniversität - has been nil, as has been its influence on the world of commercial correspondence schools.

Karl-Heinz Rebel

Rebel complains (1983:200) that 'the basis of Otto Peters' assumption - the six interdependent elements that constitute each teaching-learning process (the so-called Berlin Didactic School of Paul Heimann and Wolfgang Schulz) - could never be expressed in such a way that research data capable of falsifying this theory could be collected'.

Manfred Hamann

Hamann (1978) argues that all forms of *Zweckrationalität* whether they be called media didactics, learning psychology, systems theory, or information theory, have been without success: there have been occasional glimpses of didactic possibilities but no progress towards increased cost-efficiency in education. He accuses Peters of simply applying the structures of Heimann-Schultz to distance education and nothing more. This reproach is justifiable for only the didactical analysis part of Peters' presentation. The theory of industrialization is certainly original and owes nothing to Heimann-Schultz either in its presentation or in its origin.

Integrationist criticisms

There are critics of Peters' position who claim that he exaggerates the difference between conventional education and distance education. Many professors at the Fernuniversität would argue that learning at university level consists of extensive readings plus occasional meetings with one's professor and distance education is composed of extensive reading plus occasional meetings with a tutor.

The long tradition of German university teaching is based on learning from textual materials so that Peters' position tends to over-emphasize the difference in the communication process in distance education. Australian systems, in which numbers of students are taught on-campus and off-campus by the same lecturer, reflect a similar position. In the external studies division of the University of Queensland, for instance, each lecturer has responsibility for a defined group of students. For these students the lecturer devises the course, develops the learning materials, sees them through the production process, checks the proofs, marks the assignments for the students when enroled, provides correspondence and telephone tuition as required, may visit the students either at study centres or in their homes, and conducts the examinations.

Where, representatives of this system ask, is the division of labour, the industrialization, the mass production in this system? Where is the great role differentiation between the lecturer in a conventional and a distance system?

Peters has not replied to these critics. His most recent contribution to distance education theory (1981:47-63) merely restates his position. It implies that if he were to restate his theory today for the mid-1980s he would change only the references to economic theory and industrial analysis but would maintain the didactical structure of his position. He claims that by substituting more modern economic and industrial references he could produce a theory of the industrialization of education even more convincing than what he has achieved so far.

It is disappointing to find that the 1981 presentation repeats word-for-word the formulation of the theoretical position as it was in 1967. The positions of scholars like Ehmann, Rebel, and Hamann have not been answered.

Peters' strength is his knowledge of distance systems as they were throughout the world in the period 1960-65 and the fact that his theoretical positions are clearly grounded in the data he accumulated at that time. The theory also has a certain heuristic value, in that it offers some explanation of the nature of educational institutions in which the warehouse and the production process dominate and in which there are few educational installations and that such systems have a propensity to alienation and monopolization.

Peters' long period as foundation Vice-Chancellor of the Fernuniversität has come to an end since the publication of the first edition of this book. His present research is on the relationship of study to work in contemporary society (Peters 1984).

REFERENCES

Ehmann, C. (1981) 'Fernstudium/Fernunterricht. Reflections on Otto Peters' research', *Distance Education* 2(2), 228-33.

Hamann, M. (1978) *Fernstudienkonzeptionen für den tertiären Bildungsbereich. Analyse des Scheiterns bildungspolitischer Reformversuche in einem Teilbereich*, Hamburg: Arbeitsgemeinschaft für Hochschuldidaktik.

Heidt, E. (1978) *Instructional Media and the Individual*

Learner, London: Kogan Page.

Holmberg, B. (1982) 'Scholarship and ideology.: a study of present-day West German educational thinking', *Compare* 12(2), 133-42.

Peters, O. (1965) *Der Fernunterricht. Materialien zur Diskussion einer neuen Unterrichtsform*, Weinheim: Beltz.

Peters, O. (1967) *Das Fernstudium an Universitäten und Hochschulen. Didaktische Struktur und vergleichende Interpretation: ein Beitrag zur Theorie der Fernlehne*, Weinheim: Beltz.

Peters, O. (1968) *Das Hochschulfernstudium. Materialien zur Diskussion einer neuen Studienform*, Weinheim: Beltz.

Peters, O. (1971) 'Theoretical aspects of correspondence instruction', in O. Mackenzie and E.L. Christensen (eds) *The Changing World of Correspondence Study*, University Park and London: Penn. State.

Peters, O. (1973) *Die didaktische Struktur des Fernunterrichts. Untersuchungen zu einer industrialisierten Form des Lehrens und Lernens*, Weinheim: Beltz.

Peters, O. (1981) 'Fernstudium and industrielle Produktion. Skizze einer vergleichenden Interpretation', in P. Clever *et al.* (eds) *Okonomische Theorie und wirtschaftliche Praxis*, Herne/Berlin: Neue Wirtschaftsbriefe.

Peters, O. (1984) *Arbeit neben dem Beruf*, Hagen: Fernuniversität.

Rebel, K.H. (1983) 'Distance study in West Germany: the DIFF's conceptional contribution', *Distance Education* 4(2), 171-8.

Chapter Six

INTERACTION AND COMMUNICATION

Whatever a dead teacher may accomplish in the classroom, he can do nothing by correspondence.

William Rainey Harper, 1880

INTRODUCTION

This chapter presents writers who have emphasized interaction and communication as central to any concept of distance education. In very general terms Moore, Wedemeyer, and Delling tended to concentrate on the autonomy and independence of the student as the basis for their views, while Peters' focus is the functions of the institution developing learning materials. The authors in this chapter take as their starting point the role of the institution in providing a satisfactory learning experience for students, once the materials have been developed and dispatched.

Five authors have been selected, Bååth, Holmberg, Daniel, Sewart, and K.C. Smith. Bååth is particularly associated with an emphasis on two-way communication and Holmberg with a theory of guided didactic conversation. Daniel, Sewart, and Smith are, or have been, managers of distance systems. Their writings are developed from the day-to-day pressure of managing distance systems. Their inclusion is justified by the wide-ranging and influential character of their contributions.

TWO-WAY COMMUNICATION

John A. Bååth (pronounced 'boat') is Swedish and worked for many years for Hermods at Malmö. His work benefits from a knowledge of the literature of distance education in the Scandinavian languages, English, German, and French. During the 1970s he was associated with the concept of two-way communication in correspondence education. He would not claim to be the originator of the concept but he made an important theoretical and empirical contribution to establishing this idea as a major defining feature of distance systems today.

Table 6.1 Bååth's analysis of teaching models

Model	*Two-way communication*
B.K. Skinner's behaviour control model	Checking students' achievements; individualizing functions; assess students' starting level; consider special abilities; previous reinforcement patterns
E.Z. Rothkopf's model for written instruction	Helping students get started
D.P. Ausubel's advance organizers model	Determine each students' previous knowledge and cognitive structure; promote positive transfer to subsequent parts of course
K.Egan's model for structural communication	Individually devised discussion comments and 'reverse' assignments
J. Bruner's discovery learning model	Provide individually adapted help; stimulate students' discovery of knowledge
C. Rogers' model for facilitation of learning	Check 'open' assignments for submission; dialogue with each individual student
R.M. Gagné's general teaching model	Activating motivation; stimulating recall; providing learner guidance; providing feedback.

Source: Adapted from Bååth (1979).

One part of his research aimed to relate modern education research to distance education. He examined the applicability of the teaching models of Skinner, Rothkopf, Ausubel, Egan, Bruner, Rogers, and Gagné to correspondence education (which he regards as a subset of distance education) (1980:12).

He was able to show the functions of two-way communication in correspondence education in the light of each of the teaching models (see Table 6.1).

His conclusions are that:

- models with stricter control of learning towards fixed goals tend to imply, in distance education, a greater emphasis on the teaching material than on the two-way communication between student and tutor/institution; and
- models with less control of learning towards fixed goals tend to make simultaneous communication between student and tutor/institution more desirable; this communication taking the form of either face-to-face or telephone contacts (1979:21).

Holmberg (1981:27) summarizes Bååth's presentation of the relevance to distance education of the authorities cited in Table 6.1:

- All the models investigated are applicable to distance study.
- Some of them (Skinner, Gagné, Rothkopf, Ausubel, structural communication) seem particularly adaptable to distance study in its fairly strictly structured form.
- Bruner's more open model and even Rogers' model can be applied to distance study, though not without special measures, e.g. concerning simultaneous non-contiguous communication (telephone etc.).
- Demands on distance study systems which would inspire new developments can be inferred from the models studied.

In a second volume, *Postal Two-way Communication in Correspondence Education*, Bååth (1980) adds empirical analysis of two-way communication to the theoretical analysis of his previous book. In particular he studied:

- the relationship of submission density (frequency of assignment submission during a course) to two-way communication;
- the replacement of tutor-marked assignments by self assessment questions; and
- the introduction of computer-marked assignments as a form of two-way communication.

Bååth's theoretical and conceptual contributions stem from

his experience in Sweden. He tells us how his own situation led to his involvement:

> When writing correspondence course materials I was struck by the idea that it was possible to provide some kind of two-way communication within the material, by means of exercises, questions or self-check tests with detailed model or specimen answers. Could such two-way communication, to any considerable extent, replace the postal two-way communication induced by assignments for submission?
>
> (Bååth 1980:11-12)

This combination of personal experience and theoretical and empirical investigation led Bååth to place two-way communication as central to the distance education process and the distance tutor as central to his concept.

Bååth writes well of the importance of the tutor in a distance system. He indicates that there is evidence to show that distance learners need special help with the start of their studies and that they need help in particular to promote their study motivation (1982:22). He sees the role of the tutor going well beyond that of correcting errors and assessing students' progress:

> This is the role of the distant tutor: he can have important pedagogical functions, not only that of correcting errors and assessing students' papers. He may play a principal part in the linking of learning materials to learning - by trying to relate the learning material to each student's previous reinforcement patterns (Skinner), or to his mathemagenic activities (Rothkopf), or to his previous knowledge and cognitive structure (Ausubel), or to his previous comprehension of the basic concepts and principles of the curriculum (Bruner), or by concentrating on the task of establishing a good personal relationship with the learner (Rogers) - as I have tried to demonstrate.
>
> (Bååth 1980:121)

Bååth quotes with approval the 100-year-old statement on tutors in correspondence studies:

> The correspondence teacher must be painstaking, patient, sympathetic, and *alive*; whatever a dead teacher may accomplish in the classroom, he can do nothing by correspondence.
>
> (William Rainey Harper 1880)

A query about Bååth's work is that he does not seem to attempt a full theoretical framework for two-way communication in correspondence education. He has greatly furthered our understanding of two-way communication but has not explained how it would fit in an overview of this field.

GUIDED DIDACTIC CONVERSATION

Börje Holmberg (pronounced Burr-ye Holm-bery) is also from Sweden and today is Professor of the Methodology of Distance Education at the Fernuniversität in Hagen in the Federal Republic of Germany. He has written profusely on distance education in Swedish, German, and English.

A number of characteristic traits link together the publications of Holmberg across nearly 30 years. Among these are a generous, humanistic philosophy that values highly student independence and autonomy, an early concentration on two-way communication in distance education, an emerging concept of distance education as guided didactic conversation, a critical approach to non-print media and the provision of face-to-face sessions as components of a system and a concentration on assignment marking and its importance.

Like the dedicated humanist he is, Holmberg bases his view of distance education on his conviction that the only important thing in education is learning by individual students. Administration, counselling, teaching, group work, enrolment, and evaluation are of importance only in so far as they support individual learning. He would like to see systems with completely free pacing, a free choice of examination periods, and plenty of two-way communication for tutorial and feedback purposes.

Distance education is considered to be particularly suitable for individual learning because it is usually based on personal work by individual students more or less independent from the direct guidance of tutors. The distance student is in a situation where the chances of individually selecting what educational offerings he/she is to partake of can be much greater than that of conventional students. The student studying at a distance can, and frequently does, ignore elements of the teaching package that has been prepared for the course being studied. TV programmes or comments on assignments or face-to-face sessions or visits to study centres may all be ignored.

Holmberg characterizes study in a distance system as self-study but it is not, he insists, private reading, for the student is not alone. The student benefits from having a course developed for him and also from interaction with his tutors and other representatives of a supporting organization. The relationship between the supporting organization and the student is described as a guided didactic conversation. The general approach agrees closely with Wedemeyer's. Holmberg insists on allowing students a maximum freedom of choice in matters of both content and study procedures, individual pacing of the study, and far-reaching autonomy generally.

Two-way communication in writing and on the telephone between students and tutors has been one of his chief concerns. Students' assignments are regarded as facilitators of this communication rather than as instruments of assessment.

Distance education is seen as a guided didactic conversation that aims at learning and it is felt that the presence of the typical traits of successful conversation will facilitate learning. The continuous interaction between the student on the one hand and the tutors and counsellors and other representatives of the institution administering the study programme is seen as a kind of conversation.

There is a kind of two-way conversational traffic through the written and telephone interaction between student and institution. More dubiously Holmberg also argues for what he calls simulated conversation from the students' study of the learning materials that have been prepared in a didactic style.

Figure 6.1 Guided didactic conversation (Holmberg)

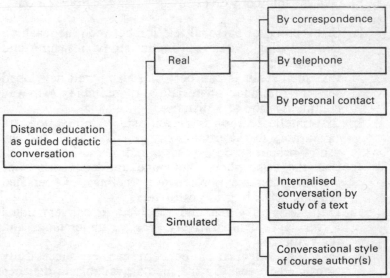

Holmberg's view of distance education as guided didactic conversation might be presented schematically as in Fig. 6.1. There are traces of these ideas in Holmberg's early writings but in recent years he has developed them into the basis for a general theory of distance education.

In *On the Methods of Teaching by Correspondence* in 1960 he wrote:

> A considerable portion of all oral tuition can rightly be described as didactive conversation. In a great number of successful correspondence courses the atmosphere and style of such conversation is found. It is typical of the style of didactive conversation that advice is given on how to tackle problems, what to learn more or less carefully, how to connect items of knowledge discussed in different lessons and this also characterises many good correspondence courses. It seems to me that advice and suggestions should preferably be expressed in phrases of personal address, such as "When you have read these paragraphs, make sure that ...".
>
> (Holmberg 1960:15-16)

The same paragraph appears with 'didactive' changed to 'didactic' in Holmberg (1967:26-7) and is repeated in *Distance Education: A Short Handbook* (1974:27-8) and in 1982 in the revised edition of that book.

Elsewhere Holmberg gives seven bases for his position:

1. that feelings of personal relation between the teaching and learning parties promote study pleasure and motivation;
2. that such feelings can be fostered by well developed self-instructional material and suitable two-way communication at a distance;
3. that intellectual pleasure and study motivation are favourable to the attainment of study goals and the use of proper study processes and methods;
4. that the atmosphere, language and conventions of friendly conversation favour feelings of personal relation according to postulate 1;
5. that messages given and received in conversational forms are comparatively easily understood and remembered;
6. that the conversation concept can be successfully translated for use by the media available to distance education;

7. that planning and guiding the work, whether provided by the teaching organisation or the student, are necessary for organized study, which is characterised by explicit or implicit goal concepts.
    (Holmberg 1978:20, repeated 1983:115-16)

Distance learning materials developed in the light of Holmberg's theory of guided didactic conversation would present the following characteristics (1983:117):

- Easily accessible presentations of study matter: clear, somewhat colloquial language, in writing that is easily readable; moderate density of information.
- Explicit advice and suggestions to the student as to what to do and what to avoid, what to pay particular attention to and consider, with reasons provided.
- Invitations to an exchange of views, to questions, to judgements of what is to be accepted and what is to be rejected.
- Attempts to involve the student emotionally so that he or she takes a personal interest in the subject and its problems.
- Personal style including the use of the personal and possessive pronouns.
- Demarcation of changes of themes through explicit statements, typographical means or, in recorded, spoken communications, through a change of speakers, e.g. male followed by female, or through pauses. (This is a characteristic of the guidance rather than of the conversation.)

If a course is prepared following these principles Holmberg (1977) forecasts that it will be attractive to students, will motivate students to study, and will facilitate learning. In two interesting experiments Holmberg re-wrote a Fernuniversität post-graduate course on educational planning and a basic Hermods course on English grammar in accordance with his theoretical position and replaced the rather analytical text-book-like approaches of the originals with a more conversational style designed to promote empathy with the student (Holmberg *et al.* 1982).

By any estimation, Holmberg's contribution to the field of distance education is extensive (1979, 1980). His early pre-occupation with two-way communication in correspondence education provided an impetus for the research of Bååth, Flinck and Wångdahl in the 1970s.

Although he is not the only scholar to recommend a

conversational style for distance learning materials he has been the only one who has developed a coherent theory from his early statement that 'a correspondence course must by definition be something different from a textbook with questions. A correspondence course provides actual teaching by itself and is thus a substitute for both a textbook and the exposition of a teacher' (1960:8) and then submitted it to empirical testing. In general this position has been beneficial to practitioners in the field and has contributed to making distance learning materials now a recognizably different genre from textbooks.

INTERACTION AND INDEPENDENCE

From 1973 to 1977 John Daniel was director of studies at the Télé-université, Université du Québec, and then Vice-President, Learning Services at Athabasca University in Edmonton, Alberta, Canada. In 1980 he took up the post of Vice-Rector (Academic) of Concordia University, a conventional university in Montreal and moved to Laurentian University, a conventional university with a small distance department in the summer of 1984.

Daniel has thus had experience of academic management in both French and English distance systems and his thinking about distance education is frequently from a management perspective.

He sees the emergence of distance education systems as coming from three sources: a long tradition of independent study; modern developments in the technology of education; and new theoretical interest in open learning. The fusion of these elements has produced new educational enterprises which teach at a distance and fulfil important economic and political needs of societies.

When Holmberg and Bååth write extensively of two-way communication in education at a distance they envisage constantly a situation in which the major part of the communication will be by postal correspondence.

Daniel (writing from the start from a university perspective) sees distance systems as comprising activities in which the student works alone and activities which bring him into contact with other people. The first grouping of activities he labels 'independent activities' and the latter 'interactive'. He provides a listing of possible activities in the two groups as in Table 6.2. A major function of distance systems is to achieve the difficult synthesis between interaction and independence

- getting the mixture right. All learning in a distance system is achieved by a balance between the learning activities the student carries out independently and those which involve interaction with other people. The balance between the two is the crucial issue facing distance study systems.

Table 6.2 Interaction and independence (Daniel)

Independent	Interactive
Reading a text	Discussion on telephone
Watching television at home	Marking and commenting on assignments
Conducting a home experiment	Group discussions
Writing an assignment	Residential summer schools

The balance chosen between the interactive and independent activities in a distance system has extensive repercussions on the administration and economics of the system. Independent activities, he tells us, have great possibilities of economies of scale since the marginal costs of printing extra copies of texts or broadcasting to more students are low. However, the cost of interactive activities tends to increase in direct proportion to the number of students (Daniel and Marquis 1979:32).

Increasing the proportion of interactive activities improves student performance but it does so at a price. The cost of interactive activities is broadly proportional to the number of students involved. There is little opportunity for the economies of scale which characterize independent activities, and which are responsible for the overall cost advantage of distance education.

Daniel states that distance systems should be dearer: things done at a distance usually are. He then parts company from much of the writing on the economics of distance education by stating that there are two economic structures for distance systems: one for the independent activities in which economies of scale are possible; and one for the interactive activities in which they may not be (Snowden and Daniel 1980).

He believes that courses should not be designed that are entirely independent. Socialization and feedback are the main functions of the interactive activities and whereas the importance of socialization in education is less vital for adults studying part-time than for children and those involved in compulsory and full-time education, the feedback role of interaction is of crucial importance. Students want to know how they are doing in relation both to their peers and to the criteria of mastery set by the course authors. Distance students are only weakly integrated into the social system of the teaching institution and feel low involvement with it. Therefore they are at risk and the importance of interactive activities is enhanced.

The thrust of Daniel's thinking on distance education comes through clearly in his attitude to pacing (Daniel and Shale 1979). He suggests that the more freedom a learner has the less likely he is to complete the course. He is of the opinion that distance systems can either give students the dignity of succeeding by pacing them or the freedom to proceed towards failure without pacing. Holmberg, on the other hand, claims that students should be free to pursue distance courses without the pressure of pacing.

Where Moore and Wedemeyer emphasize autonomy and independence of the learner studying at a distance, Daniel looks for a balance between interaction and independence in the structuring of the system and shows how this affects the pacing of students and the cost structures.

CONTINUITY OF CONCERN

David Sewart joined the Open University of the UK in 1973. After a period in the Manchester regional office he moved to the university's central site at Walton Hall near Milton Keynes where he had managerial responsibilities for the provision of support services to students. In 1980 he returned to Manchester as regional director and then returned again to Milton Keynes.

Sewart sometimes tries to trace distance education back as far as the epistles of St Paul but sees a rapid development in the last two decades. This he attributes to the new communications techniques which have been perfected in the twentieth century, the increasing costs of conventional education, and the rapidly expanding range of knowledge.

His theoretical approach to teaching at a distance can be summed up as a continuity of concern for students learning at a distance (1978). Teaching, he tells us, is a complex matter. It is an amalgam of the provision of knowledge and information plus all the advisory and supportive processes with which this provision is normally surrounded in conventional education.

He is unhappy with the notion that the package of materials in a distance system can perform all the functions of the teacher in face-to-face education. He shows that, if it could, it would become an infinitely expensive package as it would have to reflect the complex interactive process of the teacher and each individual student.

In many of his writings he discusses the efforts of course developers in distance systems to produce the 'hypothetically perfect teaching package'. He finds this unrealisable and seeks to prove this with his view of the role of the intermediary in complex civilizations. He argues that just as in most complex bureaucracies an intermediary is necessary (a social worker, a hospital orderly) to bridge the gap between the individual and the institution, so in distance systems an intermediary is necessary between the individual student and the teaching package (Fig 6.2). The intermediary is employed by the institution but works for the individuals in the system and individualizes their problems when confronted with the bureaucracy.

Figure 6.2 Role of the intermediary (Sewart)

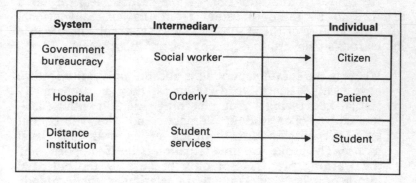

Sewart's clear emphasis on the needs of students learning at a distance, demands an interactive mode in distance systems which can hardly be supplied by the learning materials, however well they are developed. Failure to recognize this has, he considers, led to the almost universal lack of esteem for distance systems which he judges to have been the norm until quite recently. He considers that advice and support for students in a system of learning at a distance poses almost infinitely variable problems and this creates the need for an advisory and supportive role of a distance institution in addition to the provision of a teaching package.

Sewart writes of the differences between conventional and distance education and presents both the advantages and disadvantages of education at a distance. As advantages he lists:

* freedom from the 'strait-jacket of the lecture hall'
* ability to study whenever and wherever desired;
* freedom inherent in the individuality of the distance students' situation;
* student not bound by the learning pattern of a learning group; and
* distance students' needs are not subservient to the needs of a learning group.

The debits are also well presented in Sewart's writings (1981):

* no measure of progress available;
* no framework of study for the distance student;
* no peer group clarification or pressure; and
* no benchmarks on progress or failure.

He considers the situation of the student learning at a distance to be quite different from that of conventional students because of the absence of swift feedback and because the learner's peer group does not act as a benchmark.

> Whereas the infant school class and the university lecture have easily discernible differences, they are generically similar in offering a group learning situation with a face-to-face teacher/student contact, and the subsequent possibility for instant feedback of an oral and visual nature. The group learning situation is itself supportive of the learning process, not only because of the potential interaction between students in relation to the academic content of the course - learning through discussion with one's peers - but also because the group learning offers a benchmark to the individual members of the group.
>
> (Sewart 1980:177)

Sewart concludes that the process of learning at a distance is generically different from the conventional mode. The swift feedback available from the face-to-face learning model is almost entirely absent (1980:177).

The differing study patterns of distance students, the need for intermediaries in complex processes, the absence of the learning group against which the distance learner can measure himself, and the infinite variety of individual problems all lead him to the conclusion that the introduction of the human element is the only way to adapt a distance system to individual needs. This provision should ideally be available whenever and as often as the student needs it and is part of the richness and variety of a system that can adapt to the needs of individualized, independent study. Unlike Peters, however, he clearly sees all education provision as a continuum with forms of distance education fusing into conventional provision.

Sewart's views provide an effective counterbalance to those who see distance education merely as a materials production process. He claims that it is the continuity of the institution's concern for the quality of support in a distance system that has been the Open University of the UK's success in solving the age-old problem of distance systems - the avoidance of avoidable drop-out.

Sewart represents his views in an article published in 1987. There is a continuum, he tells us, between a face-to-face dialogue between one teacher and one student and a 'pure' method of teaching at a distance. There is another continuum between teaching with the complete integration of preparation and presentation by one individual at one end, and the total separation of these functions at the other (1987:163). The problem is to locate on this continuum the position of the particular distance system that one is analysing or designing.

AN INTEGRATED MODE

When the University of New England, Armidale, New South Wales, Australia began teaching externally in 1955 it adopted a system of integrating external and internal teaching by the full-time faculty of the university. External enrolments were limited on the basis of a staff-student ratio similar to that already existing in the traditional lecture situation so that staff bore responsibility for teaching both student groups as part of their normal duties.

This system (which came to be known as the 'Australian integrated mode') has had two able proponents, Howard C. Sheath (1956-72) and Kevin C. Smith (1973-84). It would be too much to say that the writings of Sheath (1965, 1973) and Smith (1979) contain a theory of distance education; rather they present a series of heartfelt beliefs on how external studies should be administered.

Smith feels that institutions planning external studies must come to terms with an educational dilemma. The dilemma lies in the fact that external studies depend essentially on an independent learning situation and must be designed so that motivated mature-age students can plot their own path through a particular course with a minimum of outside assistance. On the other hand, systems which rely solely upon the stamina, perseverance, and intellectual capabilities of students to survive the rigors of external studies without assistance do not fulfil their academic responsibilities. The compromise is to provide a core of independent learning material but to add compulsory provision for staff/student contacts and regular student group activity.

In contrast to Peters' theory of industrialization, Smith advocates dividing the work of the university faculty equally between on-campus and off-campus students. For the distance education students the lecturer performs all those functions, and more, that are performed for normal students: the design and presentation of courses, the marking of assignments, the conduct of residential and weekend schools, final assessment and examination of students. The external students enrol in the same courses, follow the same syllabus, are tutored by the same lecturers, sit for the same examinations, and are awarded the same degrees as the conventional ones.

Smith bases this structure on the following ideas (1979:31, 57):

- external teaching should not be done by part-time tutors but by the full-time university faculty;
- by being part of a normal university a distance system remains in the educational mainstream;
- a university has only a small pool of outstanding staff; external students should be in contact with them, not with what he calls 'part-time recruits';
- a university is a community of scholars and all distance students must become part of this community by attending compulsory residential schools;
- concentration on the 'learning package' can lead to a dehumanizing of the learning process, as this is a social experience;
- distance education must not depend solely on correspondence methods. Some degree of interaction not only with materials but also with other students and the teachers is essential.

Smith also lists eight beliefs about how a distance education system should be justified (1979:54):

1. *Legitimacy*: continuing education and external studies are legitimate functions of universities.
2. *Mainstream activity*: distance teaching should be undertaken by full-time academic staff as part of their normal teaching responsibilities so that it will receive the scholarship, resource allocation, and status it deserves.
3. *Commitment*: commitment is likely if the whole process remains the responsibility of the academic staff and is not divided; personal contact between academic staff and students is required; quotas are imposed to reduce external numbers to the same ratio as on-campus allocations.
4. *Parity*: parity of esteem for degrees can best be achieved if the same staff of the university teach and assess both categories of students.
5. *Interaction*: group discussions between staff and students and between students themselves are beneficial.
6. *Variety*: variety of teaching methods is recommended because of the diversity of students.
7. *Independence/pacing*: pacing of students is a characteristic of successful systems.
8. *Communication*: a distance system requires an adequate administration.

A critique of Smith's position is that he frequently puts forward the particular solutions of his own institution as normative for other institutions. The Australian integrated mode as it evolved at New England is certainly of interest as a model for a small system of less than 5,000 students, but even in other Australian universities which teach both at a distance and on-campus it has by no means been followed in all its details. Far from being in the mainstream of university studies as Smith (1979:33) claims, the distance departments of many integrated systems appear to be well on the periphery with little influence on university budgets or planning (Rothe 1987).

There is the constant problem that when a lecturer's time is divided between the demands of conventional and distance education, both functions are done less than perfectly (Shott 1983).

If an institution is offering full degrees or diplomas in a non-traditional way it does not seem appropriate that such provision should be located amongst the continuing education and extra-mural departments which do not normally offer full university degrees (Townsend-Coles (1982:29-37), yet this is where one normally finds integrated distance departments.

Nevertheless, Smith's contribution is a refreshing one. It is of value to find a thoughtful basis for rejecting concepts of mass production, cost effectiveness, and industrialization in distance education, especially when one finds emphasis placed on bringing the distance student into continuous contact with the best brains of the university and, secondly, the admission that the education of a distance student should be just as costly as a conventional one.

REFERENCES

Bååth, J. (1979) *Correspondence Education in the Light of a Number of Contemporary Teaching Models*, Malmö: Liber Hermods.

Bååth, J. (1980) *Postal Two-Way Communication in Correspondence Education* Lund: Gleerup.

Bååth, J. (1982) 'Distance students' learning - empirical findings and theoretical deliberations', *Distance Education* 3(1), 6-27.

Bååth, J., Flinck, R. and Wängdahl, A. (1975-77) *Pedagogical Reports*, Lund: University of Lund (Department of Education).

Daniel, J. and Marquis, C. (1979) 'Interaction and independence: getting the mixture right', *Teaching at a Distance* 15, 25-44.

Daniel, J. and Shale, D. (1979) 'The role of pacing in distance systems', in *The Open University Conference on the Education of Adults at a Distance*, Paper No. 9.

Harper, W.R. (1880) Cited in O. Mackenzie and B. Christensen (eds) (1971) *The Changing World of Correspondence Study*, University Park, Penn.: Penn State University.

Holmberg, B. (1960) *On the Methods of Teaching by Correspondence*, Lund: Gleerup.

Holmberg, B. (1967) *Correspondence Education*, Malmö: Hermods.

Holmberg, B. (1974) *Distance Education - A Short Handbook* Malmo: Hermods.

Holmberg, B. (1977) *Distance Education - A Survey and Bibliography*, London: Kogan Page.

Holmberg, B. (1978) 'Practice in distance education - a conceptual framework', *Canadian Journal of University Continuing Education* 6(1), 18-30.

Holmberg, B. (1979) *Fernstudiendidaktik als wissenschaftliches*

Fach, Hagen: Fernuniversität (ZIFF).

Holmberg, B. (1980) 'Aspects of distance education', *Comparative Education* 16(2), 107-19.

Holmberg, B. (1981) *Status and Trends of Distance Education*, London: Kogan Page.

Holmberg, B. (1983) 'Guided didactic conversation in distance education', in D. Sewart, D. Keegan and B. Holmberg (eds) *Distance Education: International Perspectives*, London: Routledge, pp. 114-22.

Holmberg, B. *et al.* (1982) *Zur Effizienz des gelenkten didaktischen Gespräches*, Hagen: Feruniversität (ZIFF).

Rothe, P. (1987) 'An historical perspective', in D. Kaufman and I. Mugridge (eds) *Distance Education in Canada*, London: Croom Helm.

Sewart, D. (1978) *Continuity of Concern for Students in a System of Learning at a Distance*, Hagen: Fernuniversität (ZIFF).

Sewart, D. (1980) 'Providing an information base for students studying at a distance', *Distance Education* 1(2), 171-87.

Sewart, D. (1981) 'Distance education - 'a contradiction in terms', *Teaching at a Distance* 19, 8-18.

Sewart, D. (1987) 'Staff development needs in distance education and campus-based education: are they so different?' in P. Smith and M. Kelly (eds) *Distance Education and the Mainstream*, London: Croom Helm, pp. 175-200.

Sheath, H. (1965) *External Studies at New England: The First Ten Years*, Armidale: UNE.

Sheath, H. (1973) *Report on External Studies*, Armidale: UNE.

Shott, M. (1983) 'External studies in Australia at the crossroads?' *ASPESA Newsletter* 5(2), 2-9.

Smith, K.C. (1979) *External Studies at New England: A Silver Jubilee Review*, Armidale: UNE.

Snowden, B. and Daniel, J. (1980) 'The economics and management of small post-secondary distance education systems', *Distance Education* 1(1), 68-91.

Townsend-Coles, E. (1982) *Maverick of the Education Family*, Oxford: Pergamon.

Part III

SYNTHESIS

Chapter Seven

A THEORETICAL FRAMEWORK

Distance teaching: a contradiction in terms?
David Sewart, 1981

A THEORETICAL FRAMEWORK

In this study distance education is an activity which has the following characteristics:

* quasi-permanent separation of a teacher and a learner throughout the length of the teaching process;
* quasi-permanent separation of a learner from a learning group throughout the length of the learning process;
* participation in a bureaucratized form of educational provision;
* utilization of mechanical or electronic means of communication to carry the content of the course; and
* provision of means for two-way communication so that the learner can benefit from or initiate dialogue.

Institutions which organize activities of this kind are labelled 'distance education institutions' or 'distance education departments' of other institutions. It is claimed that the characteristics outlined above render these institutions distinct from and recognizable from other institutions.

The theoretician confronted with a cluster of activities of this kind needs to address three questions:

1. Is distance education an educational activity?
2. Is distance education a conventional educational activity?
3. Is distance education possible? Is it a contradiction in terms?

Synthesis

Is distance education an educational activity?

There have been occasional suggestions that distance education does not contain any teaching function and therefore should not be classed as an educational activity. Some would wish to classify some distance education institutions with mail-order firms as a subset of business, rather than educational institutions. The data from a number of the institutions in this study showed that they were characterized by:

• input-process-output functions of an industrial rather than educational nature;
• warehousing, publishing, and dispatch as characteristic functions;
• administration by manager and clerical staff;
• 'teaching' done by accountants, bank officials, lawyers as well as school-teachers;
• institution oriented largely to production of financial profit.

In spite of these characteristics this study takes up the position that the theoretical underpinnings of distance education are to be found within general education theory. Distance education, the study claims, is a more industrialized form of education but the practice of distance education as evidenced in the second half of this book shows that the educational activities are dominant.

Is distance education a form of conventional education?

Most organized formal education is carried out in classrooms or lecture halls with an individualized teacher in person imparting knowledge and skills to a group of students. It is oral and group-based. The education imparted by such means depends on the availability of teachers at appropriate pupil/teacher ratios in appropriate buildings.

This study proposes that the basis for a theory of distance education is to be found within general educational theory but not within the theoretical structures of oral, group-based education. This is because distance education is not based on interpersonal communication and is characterized by a privatization of institutionalized learning. Thus the conclusion of O. Peters, already referred to above, is accepted: 'Anyone professionally involved in education must presume the existence of two forms of instruction which are strictly separable: traditional face-to-face teaching based on interpersonal communication and industrialized teaching which is based on a technologically-produced interaction' (1973:303).

Is distance education possible? Is it a contradiction in terms?

In the early 1970s Otto Peters set the agenda for a theoretical framework for distance education. He argued that the central theme in the study of this form of education was the justification of the abandonment of interpersonal, face-to-face communication, previously considered a cultural imperative for education in all civilizations, in favour of what Peters considered an apersonal, mechanical, or electronic 'communication' created by the technology of industrialization (Peters 1973).

Writing from UNESCO in the mid-1980s Dieuzeide commented that face-to-face communication remained a cultural imperative for education throughout the world. Distance education constitutes a fundamental break with the educational traditions of most cultures because these are based on face-to-face contact and oral communication (Dieuzeide 1985).

R.S. PETERS AND THE SCHOOL OF PHILOSOPHICAL ANALYSIS

From Otto Peters to today the search for a well-grounded theory of distance education has been an arduous one. Chapters 3-5 have presented the major contributions of scholars from various traditions. It is now time to examine distance education in the light of a generally accepted theory of education to see whether it is possible or contradictory to speak of teaching at a distance or learning at a distance.

In their 1974 book *Theories of Education. Studies of Significant Innovation of Western Educational Thought*, Bowen and Hobson claim that the English philosopher, Richard Stanley Peters, has made one of the important twentieth century contributions to the philosophy of education. Richard Stanley Peters belongs to the School of Philosophical Analysis which has been influential in educational thinking in recent decades. This group, which is represented also by Paul H. Hirst and Michael Oakeshott of the University of London Graduate School of Education, holds that the distinctive function of philosophy is analysis. They see the function of analysis as referring to both concepts and arguments and emphasize the importance of both linguistic and logical analysis.

In this study the analysis of Peters, Hirst, and Oakeshott has been chosen as a suitable basis for a theory of distance education because of the focus of this School on attempting to identify the nature of teaching and learning.

The nature of teaching

Teaching is described by this group of theorists as 'The deliberate and intentional initiation of a pupil into the world of human achievement, or into some part of it' (Oakeshott 1967) and Oakeshott explains that a pupil is a learner known to the teacher and that teaching, properly speaking, is impossible in his or her absence.

These theorists see teaching as a reciprocal act that is impossible in the absence of a learner. One cannot teach without someone being taught. In conventional, oral education this essential reciprocity is clear: if the students do not attend in the classroom or lecture hall, one can speak to the empty room - but that is not teaching. It is also clear that people learn from the day of their birth to their death and that all learning is not dependent on teaching. People learn from books, from television, from looking at the sky. Much of this learning has little to do with educational institutions, whether on-campus or at a distance. In educational analysis, nevertheless, one is concerned only with learning that is the result of communication from a teacher.

Richard Stanley Peters summarizes his views on the relationship between teaching and learning by the concept of 'intersubjectivity' between teacher and learner. In this concept learning is experienced as a conversation or a group experience. Intersubjectivity reflects a shared enterprise in which teacher and learner are united by a common zeal. He describes his concept thus:

> At the culminating stages of education there is little distinction between teacher and taught: they are both participating in the shared experience of exploring a common world. The teacher is simply more familiar with its contours and more skilled in handling the tools for laying bare its mysteries and appraising its nuances. Occasionally in a tutorial this exploration takes the form

of a dialogue. But more usually it is a group experience.
(R.S. Peters 1972:97)

Oakeshott goes further and claims that many of the important aspects of teaching cannot be taught directly. These aspects can only be learned in the presence of persons who have the qualities to be learned. 'How does a person learn disinterested zeal?', Oakeshott (1967) asks. 'How does he learn style, a personal idiom? It is implanted unobtrusively in the manner in which information is conveyed, in a tone of voice, in the gesture which accompanies instruction, in asides and oblique utterances, and by example.'

THE NATURE OF DISTANCE EDUCATION

If the position of this group of theorists has validity, is distance education a contradiction in terms? If the teaching-learning relationship is one of intersubjectivity and basically a group experience in which much is learned by association with those who have the qualities to be learned - can this take place at a distance?

An essential feature of distance education is that the teaching acts are separated in time and place from the learning acts. The learning materials may be offered to students, one, five or ten years after they were developed and to students spread throughout a nation or overseas. In distance education a teacher prepares learning materials from which he or she may never teach. Another teacher may use the materials and evaluate students' learning. The pedagogical structuring of the learning materials, instructional design, and execution may be assigned to persons other than the teacher and to persons not skilled in the content to be taught. Teaching becomes institutionalized: the course may continue in use after the lecturer responsible for producing it has died or left the institution. Materials may be developed by a course team or staff group.

Institutions which use only part-time staff may contract out the development of the teaching materials to writers who are employed only for the period of writing; tutoring and counselling are contracted out to other staff employed only for the period of the presentation of the course. All of this and much more is the day-to-day reality of teaching and learning in a distance system.

THE RE-INTEGRATION OF THE TEACHING ACTS

In spite of these realities I believe that a theoretical justification of distance education can be found. It is to be found in the attempt to re-integrate the act of teaching which is divided by the nature of distance education. The intersubjectivity of teacher and learner, in which learning from teaching occurs, has to be artificially re-created. Over space and time a distance system seeks to re-construct the moment in which the teaching-learning interaction occurs. The linking of learning materials to learning is central to this process. It may be represented schematically as in Fig. 7.1

Figure 7.1 Relationship of learning materials to learning in a distance education system

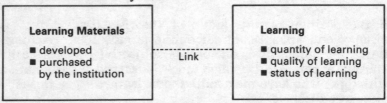

In conventional education this linking is automatically set up. It may, of course, fail if students sleep or lack motivation, but the learner is placed in a privileged situation totally geared to learning. In distance systems the position is quite different as the link between materials and potential learning has to be artificially maintained. Carefully developed distance teaching materials often fail because they are developed for and dispatched to students who do not open them, or who open them but do not study them, or who study them but do not reciprocate in any way. In a similar way distance education television or radio programmes may go unwatched or unheard, at least by the students enrolled in the course for which they were designed. The link has not been achieved; the essential reciprocity of the teaching act, shattered by the nature of distance education, has not been re-created.

INTERPERSONAL COMMUNICATION

In conventional education teacher and learner are linked by interpersonal communication which consists of language and non-verbal communication or cues. Clearly, conventional education uses textbooks and other materials in addition to interpersonal communication and as the student proceeds from primary schooling to post-graduate study the proportion of printed materials used in the learning process tends to increase. Interpersonal communication, nevertheless, remains central to the teaching-learning process and its functions may be listed as: providing information, expressing feelings, stimulating others, making social contact, controlling others, and functions related to contact seeking and role playing.

Distance education presents a cluster of educational efforts to replace these functions of interpersonal communication by printed, electronic, or computer-based interaction because the interpersonal communication of conventional education is, by definition, excluded except for occasional sessions or meetings.

Distance education has to attempt to compensate for the following differences from interpersonal communication:

- no heard language;
- absence of non-language communication (environmental factors, proxemics, kinesis, touching behaviour, para-language, physical characteristics);
- absence of feedback processes student-to-teacher;
- absence of feedback processes teacher-to-student;
- delayed reinforcement;
- absence of student-to-student communication;
- change in role of non-cognitive learning processes (peer contact, anxiety, peer support, and criticism).

Two German studies have analysed the differences between the interpersonal communication of conventional education and the artificial communication processes of distance education. Peters (1973:295) labels his analysis 'the industrialization of teaching' and Cropley and Kahl's (1983:37) study is called 'the psychodynamics of teaching at a distance'.

WHAT CAN BE ACHIEVED?

The re-integration of the teaching act is attempted by distance systems in two ways. In the first place the learning materials, both print and non-print, are designed to achieve as many of the characteristics of interpersonal communication as possible. Various writers suggest the incorporation of:

- easily readable style
- anticipation of students' problems
- careful structuring of content
- self-testing questions

- instructional objectives
- inserted questions
- model answers
- typographical considerations: designs, diagrams, and drawings.

In print, audio-visual, video, and computer packages and laboratory kits, authors try to simulate the intersubjectivity of the classroom, tutorial, or lecture.

Second, when the courses are being presented, the re-integration of the teaching act is attempted by:

- communication by correspondence
- telephone tutorials
- on-line computer communication
- comments on assignments by tutors or computers
- teleconferences, video-conferences, computer conferences.

Many institutions feel that personal contact must be available too and provide for optional or compulsory seminars, weekend meetings, or residential summer schools.

Thus distance institutions are *not* institutions for developing learning materials.

Distance education institutions seek to re-integrate the structure of teaching by providing a complete learning package that parallels the provision of conventional education institutions from pre-enrolment counselling to examination and accreditation. Distance institutions attempt to provide, as well as learning packages, as rich a structure of student support services as is possible to aid the student during the period of enrolment and study.

LE SAVOIR À DOMICILE

Having developed this analysis of distance education in the early 1980s it came as a great encouragement to find a reasonably similar approach in the 1985 book, *Le Savoir à Domicile. Pédagogie et Problematique de la Formation à Distance*, edited by Henri and Kaye. This was particularly important because it came from a different continent and from quite a different philosophical tradition.

Henri and Kaye write that 'the pedagogical act is decomposed in distance education over two periods of time and two different places'. They say that the challenge of distance education is to re-create the teaching-learning process. They describe this challenge as follows:

> The challenge which distance education attempts to take up does not lie in the teaching-learning relationship but in the way in which this relationship is achieved in the light of the distance factor. The real challenge lies in the fact that in distance education one has to re-create at a distance the teaching-learning relationship; one has to put in place from a distance an educational environment in the student's normal living milieu; that from a distance one has to plan, develop and disperse what is to be taught without the possibility of modifying it in accordance with student needs.
>
> (Henri and Kaye 1985:9)

There seems to be a reasonable similarity of analysis between the French-Canadian book and the approach adopted in this study.

THREE HYPOTHESES

In the light of the approach suggested here, three hypothetical positions can be enunciated:

1. The separation of the teaching acts and the learning acts that is characteristic of distance education brings about a weak integration of the student into the life of the institution and this has been linked to drop-out. It is hypothesized, therefore, that distance students have a tendency to drop out in those institutions in which structures for the re-integration of the teaching acts are not satisfactorily achieved.
2. The separation of the teaching acts and the learning acts that is characteristic of distance education brings about weaknesses in the achievement of interpersonal communication between teacher and student and this has been linked to the quality of the learning achieved. It is hypothesized, therefore, that distance students have difficulty in achieving quality of learning in those institutions in which structures for the re-integration of the teaching acts are not satisfactorily achieved.
3. The separation of the teaching acts and the learning acts that is characteristic of distance education places distance education among the non-traditional forms of education in which degrees, diplomas, and qualifications achieved

113

may not receive full academic acceptance. It is hypothesized, therefore, that the status of learning at a distance may be questioned in those institutions in which the re-integration of the teaching acts is not satisfactorily achieved.

CONSEQUENCES

The process of the re-integration of the act of teaching in distance education brings with it a series of changes to the normal structures of oral, group-based education. Five of the most important are considered briefly.

1. *The industrialization of teaching.* The interpersonal communication of conventional education is replaced by what are basically industrialized processes; the design of mechanical and electronic means of communication, the physical production of printed, audio, video, and computer-based materials, and the distribution of these materials throughout the territory served by the institution or throughout the world.
2. *The privatization of institutional learning.* The learning group is splintered and students study, basically at home, throughout the territory served by the institution. Teaching is focused on the individual student who does not, however, study as a private learner but as a member of an often complex educational bureaucracy.
3. *Change of administrative structure.* Distance institutions are characterized by two characteristic operating sub-systems which have specific task and psychological boundaries: course development subsystem and student support services subsystem.
4. *Different plant and buildings.* The warehouse is central, together with postal or other distribution services. Greatly reduced or spread throughout the territory are student facilities ranging from seminar rooms to library and laboratory facilities.
5. *Changes of costing structures.* Distance systems are characterized by high initial start-up costs, lower variable costs per student and give the potential for significantly lower average costs per student provided the student population is large enough. This represents a move away from the labour-intensive costs of education towards the capital investment structures of industrial enterprises.

REFERENCES

Bowen, J. and Hobson, H. (1974) *Theories of Education. Studies of Significant Innovation in Western Educational Thought*, London: Methuen.

Cropley, A. and Kahl, T. (1983) 'Distance education: a psychological analysis', *Distance Education* 4(1), 30–42.

Dieuzeide, H. (1985) 'Les enjeux politiques', in F. Henri and A. Kaye (eds) *Le Savoir à Domicile*, Québec: Téléuniversité, 29–60.

Henri, F. and Kaye, A. (eds) (1985) *Le Savoir à Domicile* Québec: Téléuniversité.

Oakeshott, M. (1967) 'Learning and teaching', in R.S. Peters (ed.) *The Concept of Education*, London: Routledge & Kegan Paul.

Peters, O. (1973) *Die didaktische Struktur des Fernunterrichts*, Weinheim: Beltz.

Peters, R.S. (1972) 'Education as initiation', in R. Achambault, (ed.) *Philosophical Analysis and Education*, London: Routledge & Kegan Paul.

Sewart, D. (1981) 'Distance teaching: a contradiction in terms?' *Teaching at a Distance* 19, 8–18.

Chapter Eight

A TYPOLOGY OF DISTANCE TEACHING SYSTEMS

There are distance teaching universities only in South
Africa and the USSR.

Otto Peters, 1965

BACKGROUND

It used to be accepted that distance teaching started in 1840.
Holmberg (1960:3) gives that as the date when Isaac Pitman
offered tuition by post in shorthand to students in England. In
1856 Charles Toussaint and Gustave Langensheidt commenced
language teaching by correspondence in Germany. Delling
(1979:13), however, has argued convincingly that institutions
which exhibit all the characteristics suggested in Chapter 3 are
little more than a century old.

Today a listing of distance institutions would embrace
most countries of the world and all levels of education.

In previous chapters an attempt has been made to delineate
and characterize what has been called 'the farrago that is
distance education: open universities and schools of the air;
TV and radio projects; government-sponsored institutions
prohibited by statute from charging fees alongside profit-
making colleges; literacy and rural improvement projects;
computer-based instruction and instruction based on roneoed-
notes'.

A stringent listing of systemic characteristics has been
proposed whereby only those institutions exhibiting certain
academic and administrative peculiarities, which are reflected
in decisions about physical plant, are considered to be distance
education institutions for the purpose of this study. Even then
the field remaining is vast (Harry 1984) and there is great
variety of provision. Global statements about distance
education as a whole are rarely valid and most general

statements must be hedged with qualifications. The need to provide the reader with groupings or classifications about which at least some general statements may be made with confidence is pressing.

In this chapter some existing classifications which contain elements that contribute to an understanding of the field of distance education are discussed, then a new classification, specially prepared for this study, is suggested.

EXISTING TYPOLOGIES

O. Peters (1971)

The first systematic classification of distance institutions at higher education level is provided by Peters' *Texte zum Hochschulfernstudium*. Peters proposes two major groupings: a western model based on printed materials and correspondence feedback and an eastern model based on printed materials and regular face-to-face sessions. Four bases are given by Peters (1971:8-12) for his classification: political structure, curriculum structure, organizational structure, and didactic structure (see Table 8.1).

Peters' view that there are two basic forms of distance provision: an eastern one based on printed materials plus consultations and a western one based on printed materials plus correspondence feedback was not followed by the two other major comparative studies of distance education published in the 1970s. Both the UNESCO *Open Learning* (McKenzie *et al.* 1975) study and the Swedish TRU report (1975) saw broadcast radio and television as central.

J. El Bushra (1973)

El Bushra, of the International Extension College in Cambridge, developed a classification of correspondence teaching at universities, comprising the six categories given in Table 8.2. This presentation contains elements of value for an understanding of university distance provision, though a number of groupings chosen are too small for valid use.

Table 8.1 Typology of O. Peters

	Western models *(pp.29–139)*	*Eastern models* *(pp.143–229)*
Political considerations	Tries to help the individual	A planned component of of socio-cultural development
	Is a fringe form of educational provision	An integral part of national provision
	Characterized by proprietary influences	Enrols 20–50% of all undergraduates
Curriculum	Fragmented provision from individual institutions	Centralized national provision
Organizational structure	Loosely integrated into the mainstream of university life	More influential role in university structures
Didactic structure	Based on proprietary precedents: mono-media system of printed materials plus regular correspondence correction of assignments	Based on imitation of direct education: correspondence correction of assignments is reduced or replaced by regular voluntary or compulsory seminars
Examples in 1971	Wisconsin and Nebraska (USA) New England (Australia) UNISA (South Africa) Chuo, Hosei, Kaio (Japan) Open University (UK)	Karl-Marx, Leipzig (GDR) Karls, Prague (Czechoslovakia) North Western Polytechnic, Leningrad (USSR) Poland and Peoples Republic of China

Source: Adapted and translated from Peters (1971)

Table 8.2 Typology of J. El Bushra

Type	Examples
1. Universities dealing exclusively with external students	UNISA, OUUK
2. Universities offering external examination facilities only	External degrees of the University of London
3. Universities offering correspondence teaching in one department only	College of Estate Management (University of Reading) and School of Education; University of the South Pacific
4. Universities in which teaching departments are required to accept both internal and external students	University of New England
5. Universities in which external teaching is provided in a separate department	University of Queensland External Studies Department; University of Wisconsin Extension
6. Universities collaborating to provide instruction on a co-operative basis	Massey University, New Zealand; Texas Association for Graduate Engineering and Research (TAGER)

Source: Adapted from El Bushra (1973).

M. Neil (1981)

Neil of the Open University of the UK presents a classification of distance institutions based on (i) the degree of authority and (ii) the degree of control exerted by the various types of distance institutions in key operational areas (1981:138-41). The key operational areas are:

- finance
- examination and accreditation
- curriculum and materials
- delivery and student support services.

Synthesis

Neil states that an autonomous distance teaching university is a 'whole system control model' with control and authority over the four operational areas listed. Distance departments which are not autonomous but subsections of other institutions are 'embedded into communities of educational agencies' for the purpose of mutual benefits. These 'mixed' models have to share both control and authority in the four key operational areas (1981:130).

Table 8.3 Typology of M. Neil

Title	Description	Example
1. Classical centre-periphery model	Whole system control model	OUUK, Milton Keynes
2. Associated centre	An autonomous university with centralized control diminished in area of financing and support services	Universidad Nacional de Educación a Distancia, Madrid
3. Dispersed centre model	An autonomous institution which co-operates with a wide variety of institutions	Coastline Community College, California
4. Switchboard organization model	A facilitating centre for distance education projects with much control exercised by other educational and public bodies	Norsk fjernundervisnung, Norway
5. Service institution model	A service institution based on co-operation with other institutions	DIFF, Tübingen

Source: Adapted from Neil (1981).

Table 8.4 Typology of Chester Zelaya Goodman

Title and description	Example
1. Private institutions providing distance teaching for a.public institution	Wolsley Hall, Oxford; National Extension College, Cambridge
2. Conventional universities which offer distance course which they also accredit	Universidad Nacional Autonoma de Mexico; Universidad Xavariana, Bogotà
3. Groupings of conventional universities which unite to offer distance courses	Entente de l'est, France; DIFF, Tübingen
4. Autonomous multi-level distance institutions which teach at university level	Centre National d'Enseignement par Correspondance,France
5. Universities specially created to offer and accredit degrees at a distance	OUUK; UNED, Spain; UNA, Venezuela; UNED, Costa Rica

Source: Adapted from Zelaya (no date).

Autonomous distance education institutions clearly have relationships with other education institutions in the nation or state and Neil characterizes these relationships as contractual or commercial. By contrast, distance education departments are embedded in other systems so that mutual benefit between sectors is an important bond.

Chester Zelaya Goodman

The two volume Peñalver-Escotet analysis of distance education *Teoria y Praxis de la Universidad a Distancia* contains a typology of distance systems by Chester Zelaya Goodman in his chapter 'La admistración de los sistemas de educación a distancia y sus costos' (no date: 141-57) as shown in Table 8.4. This is a well-informed and carefully presented typology of distance systems at university level. The reader will notice how Zelaya accommodates within his structure both the correspondence schools which teach at a distance towards University of London degrees and the co-operative ventures in eastern

Table 8.5 Typology of Keegan and Rumble

	Name	*Description*	*Examples*
1.	Autonomous, centrally controlled distance teaching universities	Open universities with centralized, autonomous structures	OUUK; EU; AU; UNED, Costa Rica
2.	Autonomous, decentralized distance teaching universities	Open universities with some devolution of powers	UNED, Spain
3.	Essentially autonomous distance teaching universities operating within a federated university structure	Federal university with both conventional universities and a distance teaching unit	Télé-université of the federal University of Québec
4.	Autonomous centralized distance teaching system with a high degree of control using facilities based in and run by conventional universities	Ministry control of distance education departments within conventional universities	Central Office for Distance Education, Dresden, GDR
5.	Mixed-mode, uni-departmental model	Special academic distance teaching department in conventional university	External Studies Department, University of Queensland
6.	Mixed-mode, multi-departmental model	Academic staff responsible for both internal and external students	Australian integrated mode, New England model
7.	Mixed-mode, multi-institutional model	Mixed-mode with responsibility for students at other universities	Massey University, New Zealand

Source: Adapted from Keegan and Rumble (1982).

France, now restructured, and from Tübingen.

Zelaya's category 'conventional universities which offer distance courses which they also accredit' can easily accommodate the sixty-four independent study departments of US universities, the similar structures in Canada, and external studies provision from Swedish and Australian universities. The decision to separate out the CNEC in France as a major provider in an autonomous multi-level distance system is quite justified.

He calls his final grouping the SEAD (Sistemas de Educación a Distancia) and claims that these institutions are totally dedicated to external students. The characteristics are absence of conflicts of loyalty on the part of academic staff between on-campus and off-campus students, greater motivation for methodological experiment; freedom from conventional academic traditions; and - in general - ability to develop new educational initiatives for new target groups.

D. Keegan and G. Rumble (1982)

In the preparation of the book *The Distance Teaching Universities*, Keegan and Rumble wrestled with the problem of the classification of distance systems at university level and came up with the seven basic organizational structures listed in Table 8.5.

CONDITIONS FOR A VIABLE TYPOLOGY

The classification in this study is based on the following premises for the construction of a usable typology:

- It should be helpful to the readers, enabling them to focus on a range of institutions within the field 'distance teaching institutions' about which statements can be made that identify what this grouping of institutions has in common, and what it is that distinguishes it from the other groupings.
- To be helpful it should not be artificial - each grouping should contain dozens, preferably hundreds, of institutions.
- It should not be artificial with regard to students - each grouping should enrol thousands, preferably millions, of students.
- It should not be artificial with regard to time - each grouping should have been identifiable for at least a

decade, preferably longer.

- It should try to encompass all distance teaching institutions, public and private, at all levels from primary schooling to post-graduate levels – and not just concentrate on distance education at university level.
- It should only include those distance teaching institutions or departments of existing institutions which exhibit both the major characteristic subsystems of distance institutions (course development and student support services) – for without this limitation the variants are legion. Institutions or departments which are considered not to exhibit both these operational subsystems are excluded (though some of them have made excellent contributions to distance education).

Fundamental to the classification proposed here is the acceptance (with Neil, Keegan, and Rumble) that the basic distinction is between *autonomous distance teaching institutions* and *distance subsections of conventional institutions* (Fig. 8.1). As an explanation of 'autonomous' Neil's (1981:140) listing of autonomy in (i) finance, (ii) examination and accreditation, (iii) curriculum and materials, and (iv) delivery and student support systems, is accepted as accurate.

Figure 8.1 Typology of distance teaching institutions

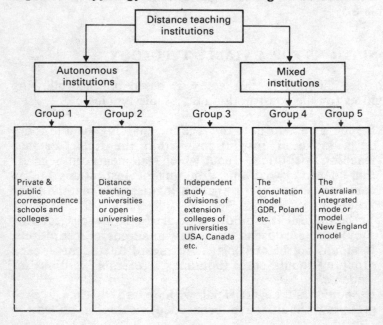

It is a question of autonomy at the institutional level because autonomous distance institutions like the Open University of the UK, the Centre National d'Enseignement à Distance in France, and the New South Wales College of External Studies in Australia are components of state or national education systems. Neil explains: 'Although the OUUK is enmeshed in, and utterly dependent upon, the United Kingdom infrastructure, its relationships with other organizations are basically contractual and commercial in nature' (1981:139).

Once these two basic groupings have been established, further division within the two groupings is by didactic structure, that is the linking structures that the groupings of institutions provide between learning materials and learning. It is when institutions are classified in this way that it starts to become possible to make general statements about the groupings that have some validity. Distance education is too rich and diversified a field of education for more general statements of the type 'all distance institutions do this' to be possible without so many nuances and qualifications as to be virtually unintelligible.

AUTONOMOUS DISTANCE TEACHING INSTITUTIONS

The autonomous distance teaching institutions have been divided into two groups for the purpose of this study. Group 1 is called 'Public and private correspondence schools and colleges' and Group 2 'Distance teaching universities'. The division between the two groups is based on complexity of didactic structure and level of provision.

In very general terms the link between learning materials and learning provided by Group 1 institutions tends to be less complex than by those of Group 2, especially in the use of 'big media' (Schramm 1977) and face-to-face meetings. Group 1 institutions, whether public or private, sometimes state that students enrol with them precisely because they wish to avoid face-to-face contact. Group 2 institutions sometimes have the intention of supporting the distance learner by as rich a provision of support services as possible.

In terms of level of provision Group 1 institutions normally provide courses for children and adults at lower than university level. Group 2 institutions are called distance teaching universities. The division is not watertight, however, as many Group 1 institutions offer some university level courses, while most distance teaching universities offer courses below university level.

Autonomous distance teaching institutions that provide a full range of courses from basic adult education to university programmes are of particular importance. Rather than create a new category for these multi-level providers they will be regarded here as having a mixture of characteristics from the two groupings identified.

Public and private correspondence schools and colleges (Group 1)

Correspondence schools and colleges are autonomous distance teaching institutions. They control or have authority over staffing, finance, accreditation, development of materials, and student services even when they are part of a state-wide or nation-wide system.

This model is used widely throughout the world both by government-sponsored and by proprietary institutions. Schools and colleges of this type have existed for over 100 years and today there are examples in nearly every country of the western world. Examples are found particularly amongst government-sponsored schools at primary and secondary level, and both publicly sponsored and privately supported colleges at technical, vocational, and further education levels. Some well-known examples are the National Extension College, Cambridge; Leidse Onderweijsinstellingen, Leiden and the New South Wales College of External Studies, Sydney. In Australia, Canada, and New Zealand this has been the chosen model for government correspondence schools for nearly 70 years, with the Alberta Correspondence School, founded in 1923, reaching 60,330 annual enrolments by 1986 (Turnbull 1987:108). Karow (1979) listed 144 Group 1 institutions (all proprietary) in the Federal Republic of Germany and there must be at least as many in France.

Group 1 is an institutional structure which emphasizes the correspondence element in distance education. It might be represented diagrammatically as in Fig. 8.2. The didactic structure is frequently patterned thus: the correspondence schools and colleges develop or purchase learning materials and send them by post to the student. The student studies the materials and posts assignments back to the institution which marks and comments on them and posts them back to the student. The student studies the comments, completes the next assignment and the process is repeated.

Figure 8.2 A correspondence school or college model (Group 1)

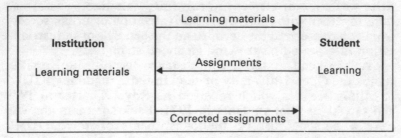

Print tends to be the didactic medium with some use of audio cassettes. From this description and the diagrammatic representation in Fig. 8.2 it can be indicated that the environment for student learning provided by this model can be fragile. The student's main contact with the representatives of the institution is by post so that isolation can become a problem.

As many correspondence schools and colleges have a philosophy that suggests that students enrol with them because 'they want to be left alone', it can be maintained that student support services and face-to-face sessions can infringe learner autonomy or the independence of the adult learner. Gone are peer group support and the presence of the teacher. Drop-out can be enormous.

There are, nevertheless, institutions which have turned these disadvantages into factors to benefit student learning. There is evidence to claim (Bååth and Wångdahl 1976; Bååth 1979; Rekkedal 1981; Holmberg 1981:83-94) that the dedication of the correspondence tutor can forge with the distant student by letter and by telephone such a creative link that a correspondence course can become a form of privileged one-to-one study. A type of one-on-one bonding has often been created that is difficult to achieve in lecture or tutorial.

Distance teaching universities (Group 2)

In 1965 Otto Peters wrote 'The Republic of South Africa and the USSR are the only countries with distance teaching universities'. The scene was quite different 20 years later.

Distance education started the decade of the 1970s as the Cinderella of the education spectrum: it was practically unknown as a segment of national education provision and at times criticized for the malpractice of some of its representatives. It emerged in the 1980s with the possibility of a radical change of image. The foundation of the open universities was a major element in this fairy-tale like transformation, together with the growing privatization of urban society which characterized the decade and the benefits of industrialization in a period of growing financial stringency.

At the head of the list of distance teaching universities stands the Open University of the United Kingdom (OUUK) at Milton Keynes which received its Royal Charter in 1969 and taught its first students in 1971. Each commentator will have a personal list of the constituents of the OUUK's immediate success, but amongst them were brilliant political and educational leadership, an unswerving concentration on the needs of students studying at a distance and a national backlog of intelligent adults for whom the provisions of face-to-face universities were not fully relevant. These factors and others quickly brought this non-traditional university structure the status of a permanent provider of university education in the UK with an annual enrolment of 100,000.

The OUUK was followed by a series of foundations in both developed and developing countries of similar institutions called 'Fernuniversitäten', 'open universities' or 'universidades de educación a distancia'. Not only does the foundation of these universities mark a watershed in distance education, it provides the most advanced stage yet in the evolution of the concept of a university.

These universities do not have students in residence, neither do they have full-time day-time students, nor even part-time night-time students. They place their students at home. One looks in vain for students as one walks around the campus at Milton Keynes. Many of the other universities are off-putting, factory-like buildings and there is little or nothing for students to do at them. Gone too is the concept of the university library with places for undergraduate and post-graduate research, gone are the lecture rooms, tutorial rooms, seminar rooms, laboratories for student research, and facilities for the student community.

These are universities of a nation or a state, not of a city like Oxford or Bologna. Frequently they are universities on tens or hundreds of sites spread throughout the nation.

These universities present the most radical challenge yet to the idea of a university enunciated by John H. Newman and developed in the western world. They represent the final democratization of the concept of a university by opening up the possibility of university studies to many who were formerly barred from enroling by the timetabling of lectures and the necessity of set periods of research at the universities' facilities.

Full-time workers, the disabled, imprisoned, and hospitalized together with those tied to the home can now enrol at a university if it teaches at a distance.

In didactic structure, Group 2 institutions attempt to provide a more comprehensive linking between learning materials and student learning. This might be represented as in Fig. 8.3.

Figure 8.3 A distance teaching university model (Group 2)

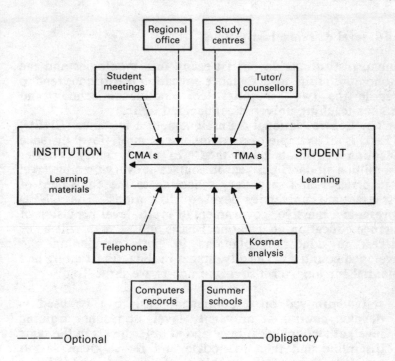

————Optional   ———Obligatory

Distance teaching universities differ from Group 1 institutions in three ways: 1. the level of provision; 2. the use of media; and 3. the more comprehensive link between learning materials and potential learning.

1. *The level of provision.* Correspondence schools and colleges in Group 1 concentrate on education for school children and further education for adults. The distance teaching universities focus on the provision of university degrees at a distance, though most of the group offer further

education courses as well.

2. *The use of media.* A study by Keegan and Rumble (1982:213) shows a movement towards a more extensive use of educational media by the distance teaching universities. In general Group 2 institutions make a more comprehensive use of non-print educational media than Group 1 institutions.

3. *The didactic link.* Group 2 institutions profess to provide a more coherent link between learning materials and learning so that a satisfactory university level educational experience is provided.

Multi-level distance institutions

Human institutions do not fit easily into typologies and the autonomous multi-level distance education institutions tend to straddle the two groupings (correspondence schools and distance teaching universities) decided upon.

The Centre National d'Enseignement à Distance (CNED) in Paris is an example of an autonomous multi-level distance education institution. Today the CNED enrols nearly a quarter of a million students per year in courses at every possible level from primary and secondary schooling to the equivalent of post-graduate university level qualifications. The CNED represents a massive, governmental, multi-level provision of distance education on a national basis and as such will be of interest to education planners in both developing and developed countries. The advantages in didactic structure and potential for long-term savings in costs are three-fold:

- staff employed on a permanent basis can be used to develop courses at university level, at teacher training level, at technological level and at other levels in the same discipline and then to update and revise them - thus avoiding some of the problems of tenured academics in Group 2 institutions;
- staff employed as lay-out artists, audio and video programmers, and instructional designers can benefit from skills learned from working on courses at various levels; and
- instructional designers and plant for media production are all provided once to the same institution and the system does not have to duplicate these installations and staff for each sector's distance departments or institutions.

This model has had at least one important parallel in recent years: the Open Learning Institute at Richmond, British Columbia - a suburb of Vancouver. The Government of British Columbia set up in 1979 an autonomous three-level distance teaching institution to complement a range of small providers of university study by correspondence through departments in conventional universities (see Group 3, p.132).

Figure 8.4 Open Learning Institute, British Columbia to 1986 (a multi-level model)

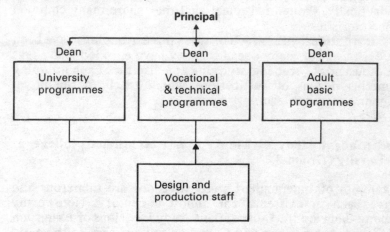

Figure 8.4 presents the structure of the Open Learning Institute prior to 1986. A restructure in that year preserved the elements of a multi-level provision, serviced by a single production and design unit. This structure provided a full range of distance programmes for adults within the one institution ranging from literacy/numeracy, through a wide range of technical/vocational community college programmes, to the availability of university degrees. All three levels shared the same production facilities, the same course development and instructional design expertise and the same student support services.

DISTANCE EDUCATION DEPARTMENTS OF CONVENTIONAL INSTITUTIONS

For the purpose of this study three types of a distance education department or section within the structures of a conventional institution have been distinguished. These are:

- independent study divisions of a conventional college or university (Group 3);
- distance education departments of institutions in the socialist republics of Central and Eastern Europe - the consultation model (Group 4); and
- the Australian integrated mode - New England model (Group 5).

It is felt that these three groupings can be satisfactorily distinguished one from the other both administratively and didactically, though it is clear that they share many common characteristics.

Institutions within each of these three groupings have been in existence for many decades. They have enrolled many tens of thousands of students studying at a distance. Each grouping contains dozens of institutions which teach, normally, at higher education level.

Independent study divisions of a conventional college or university (Group 3)

Examples of independent study divisions are numerous and have been in existence for almost a century. Noteworthy among them are the Independent Study Divisions of Extension Colleges of American and Canadian universities. In the early 1980s, sixty-four American universities had independent study departments and there were twenty similar structures in Canada. In France the Centres de Télé-enseignement Universitaire (CTUs) at nearly twenty universities fall within this category. In Sweden distance education is organized in this way from a number of Swedish universities. Many universities in India and Latin America have correspondence or distance departments within this category.

Recent studies have been published of a number of these institutional arrangements, notably by Markowitz (1983) on the independent study departments of United States universities, by Willén (1983) on distance education in Swedish universities, by Escotet (1980) on the Latin American provision, and by Singh (1980) and Carr (1983) on India.

One of the administrative structures of these universities is the Continuing Education or Extension College. The Department of Independent Study or Correspondence Study is usually one of the divisions of the Extension College. Departments of Independent Study offer courses in ten major delivery modes within the field of distance education:

Correspondence lessons
Credit by examination
Contract alternative
Directed individual study
Special programmes for groups
Television courses
Video cassette courses
Radio courses
Audio cassette courses
University without walls.

Course development is usually by university faculty paid overload to produce the courses, though a smaller number of faculty (called adjunct faculty) come from other universities, and occasionally from other sectors of the academic community. Tuition is also provided by the university faculty and the students study for degrees or certificates awarded by the university. However, there are limitations on the use of independent study credits for degree programmes in certain departments or schools of the university, and in many cases, one is not permitted to complete a full degree by independent study.

The consultation model (Group 4)

Peters' (1971) classification of two basic structures for distance education, print-based with correspondence feedback in the west and print-based with consultations in the east, was a valid analysis of distance education in the 1960s and still has its uses today. In this study, however, the autonomous distance teaching universities of the USSR are placed in Group 2 (the distance teaching universities) and a special category (Group 4) is created for the consultation model when it is a subset of a mixed institution which teaches both on-campus and at a distance.

The consultation model has been documented for the German Democratic Republic by Schwartz (1978), Möhle (1978), and Dietze (1979), for the USSR by Gorochov (1979) and Ilyin (1983), for Bulgaria by Christow and Mutojischiew (1979), for Hungary by Fekete and Nahlik (1979), and for Yugoslavia by Krajnc (1988).

The didactic model of Group 4 is quite different from western systems and 'correspondence' usually plays little role in it. In some systems students, on enrolment, are allocated both to the institution from which they will get their degree (which may be far away) and to a consultation centre at an institution near to their home and work. In other systems the enrolment and the consultation centre are at the same university.

Study commences with a residential seminar on-campus. After this students study at home from the learning materials provided. This home study is interspersed at regular intervals (often once a fortnight) by consultations which are frequently compulsory. A consultation consists of a day's work on-campus in which the student receives face-to-face guidance in each of the subjects being studied.

The consultation model highlights characteristics of distance education that are not found, or are not found so clearly in Groups 1, 2, 3, and 5. Amongst these are:

- Distance education is seen as a democratization of educational provision by opening up to all adults, irrespective of their place of work, access to university qualifications at all levels.
- Distance education provides for the nation a means of training the workforce without withdrawing students from contributing to the Gross National Product throughout the length of their studies.
- Distance education is linked to the students' work and there is constant interaction between work and study.
- Of the major types of distance education provision it is the one which is closest to face-to-face provision.

Ilyin (1983) gives a presentation of the consultation model in the USSR. Apart from the fourteen distance teaching universities (classified as Group 2 institutions in this study), he refers to no fewer than '800 distance subsidiaries and branches of full-time universities and institutes'.

In the German Democratic Republic the ratio of face-to-face consultations to individual study at home is 20 per cent as the 1:1 rhythm of equal attendance on-campus and private study expected of conventional students is replaced by a 5:1 rhythm in *Fernstudium*. A typical study programme for the first semester of the first year of an engineering degree at a distance shows this ratio as in Table 8.6.

Besides the learning materials there are three other major components of the didactic structure: private study, the students' workplace, and regular seminars (consultations). The students' workplace plays an important role in the study programme. Students are usually sponsored by their firm. They receive by law 48 days paid study leave per year. Their thesis is usually on some aspect of the company's product or management. They are, in effect, practically guaranteed a promotion position upon graduation.

Table 8.6 Structure of degree in engineering in German Democratic Republic

Distance Engineering (Transport) Degree: Semester 1		
Subject	Self-study time (hours)	Consultations (hours)	Lectures (hours)
Marxism-Leninism	50	10	2
Russian	80	15	14
Mathematics	135	30	4
Physics	85	14	2
Materials technology	50	10	2
Total	400	80	36

Source: Adapted and translated from Dietze (1979).

Schwartz (1978) and Möhle (1978) present the didactic structure schematically as in Fig. 8.5. It is claimed that this interaction of work and study provides a unique blending of theoretical and practical learning that is not paralleled in ordinary education.

The Australian integrated mode - New England model (Group 5)

A distinct form of distance education department within a conventional college or university has evolved in Australia. It is known as the 'New England model' (New England is an area in New South Wales, 300 km NW of Sydney) or the 'Australian integrated mode'. It has been extensively presented: Sheath (1965, 1973), Smith (1979, 1984), Ortmeier (1981), Laverty (1980), Dahllöf (1978), Guiton (1981), White (1982), Shott 1983a, b). It is found, with variations, in Australian colleges of advanced education and universities that teach at a distance. Systems in Zambia, Fiji, Papua New Guinea, and Jamaica have been modelled on it.

Figure 8.5 A consultation system model (Group 4)

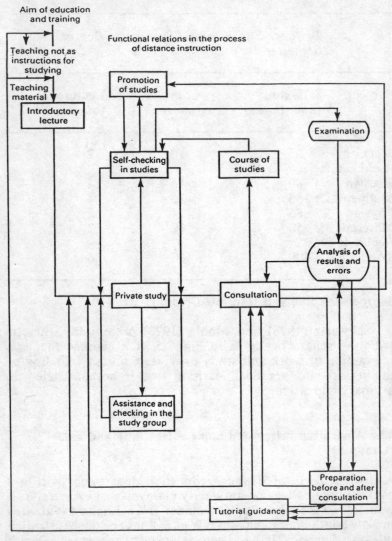

Source: Adapted and translated from Schwarz (1978), Möhle (1978)

Figure 8.6 Australian integrated mode model (Group 5)

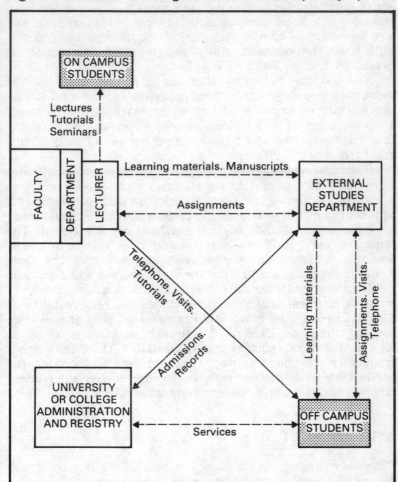

There had been a long history of distance education in Australia prior to the founding of the University of New England at Armidale in 1955, but all from Group 1 or Group 3 structures. Individual Australian universities or colleges do not have sufficient distance students to warrant the foundation of an autonomous institution.

In 1955 the University of New England commenced teaching both on-campus and externally. A unique staffing structure and an attempt to preserve as much of on-campus provision for students as possible was evolved for the distance system. The university's lecturers were given a dual mandate

137

and allocated groups of both internal and external students in equal numbers. Lecture notes and even audio-cassette tapes recorded live in on-campus lectures were sent to students and a requirement of compulsory periods of time on-campus was built into the distance study programme. This model is presented schematically in Fig. 8.6.

The system maintains that the academic staff of the university or college are to be responsible for the total teaching/learning process of writing courses, teaching them through a combination of independent study materials and face-to-face tuition and assessing the students by way of assignments and formal examinations.

The external studies department is therefore an administrative one which organizes for students a series of interactive activities, including at least a brief period of traditional university or college life as a full-time student in residence.

Thus external and internal teaching are integrated. The same academic staff teach and assess both sets of students. Students are enrolled in the same courses, take the same examinations, and qualify for the same degrees and diplomas.

Because academic staff have internal teaching commitments to conventional students, besides the responsibility of developing learning materials for external studies and then tutoring them, an External Studies Department is set up to relieve them of administrative details. This department frequently has no teaching function but looks after the production and distribution of course material, student records, statistics, and student support services.

OTHER STRUCTURES

Distance education institutions, as defined in this book, are institutions which teach students. They parallel ordinary schools, colleges, and universities in that they enrol students, teach, assess, and evaluate them and provide a total learning experience for them in every way. They also have a second function, which is not paralleled by ordinary schools, colleges, and universities. They prepare for (some scholars would use the verb 'teach' here too) future students. They prepare printed, audio, video, and/or computer-based learning materials for students who will enrol in the future - next year or in 2-10 years in the future.

The demands of a viable typology that would comprise groupings of institutions large enough for practical use has eliminated from consideration a number of institutions that are often associated with the evolution of distance education. These include (i) some accrediting institutions; (ii) some materials production centres; and (iii) certain audio-video and television programmes.

CONCLUSION

In this chapter a classification has been provided for those institutions characterized by all the characteristics of distance education institutions outlined in the previous chapters. Within the unity of distance education, a major difference was claimed between autonomous distance education institutions and distance departments of conventional institutions. Within these two groupings further subdivisions were indicated to arrive at groupings of institutions about which general statements can be made with confidence.

REFERENCES

Bååth, J. (1979) *Postal Two-Way Communication in Correspondence Education*. Malmö: Liber Hermods.

Bååth, J. and Wangdähl, A. (1976) 'The tutor as an agent of motivation in correspondence education', *Pedagogical Reports*, No. 8, University of Lund.

Carr, R. (1983) 'Distance education in Indian universities: a change of direction?' *Distance Education* 4(2), 101-19.

Childs, G. (1971) 'The University of Nebraska Independent Study Division', in O. Peters, *Texte zum Hochschulfernstudium*, Weinheim: Beltz, pp. 57-70.

Christow, J. and Mutojischiew, L. (1979) 'Die Entwicklung des Fernstudiums in der Volksrepublik Bulgarien', in G. Deitze (ed.) *IVe Internationales Wisenschaftliches Seminar zum Hochschulfernstudium*, Dresden: Zentralstelle für das Hochschulfernstudium des Ministeriums für Hoch- und Fachschulwesens, pp. 22-30.

Dahllöf, U. (1978) *Reforming Higher Education and External Studies in Sweden and Australia*, Stockholm: Almquist & Widsell.

Delling, R. (1979) Lehrbrief als Fernlehrgelegenheit, *ZIFF Papiere*, Hagen: Fernuniversität.

Dietze, G. (ed.) (1979) *IVe Internationales Wisenschaftliches Seminar zum Hochschulfernstudium*, Dresden: Zentralstelle für das Hochschulfernstudium des Ministeriums für Hoch- und Fachschulwesens.

El Bushra, J. (1973) *Distance Teaching at University Level*, Cambridge: IEC.

Escotet, M. (1980) 'Adverse factors in the development of an open university in Latin America', in D. Sewart, D. Keegan and B. Holmberg (eds) (1983) *Distance Education: International Perspectives*, London: Croom Helm.

Fekete, J. and Nahlik, J. (1979) 'Ungarn', in G. Deitze (ed.) *IVe Internationales Wisenschaftliches Seminar zum Hochschulfernstudium*, Dresden: Zentralstelle für das Hochschulfernstudium des Ministeriums für Hoch- und Fachschulwesens, pp. 31-44.

Gorochov, W.A. (1979) 'Hauptwege zur Verrollkommung des Fernstudiums in der USSR', in G. Deitze (ed.) *IVe Internationales Wisenschaftliches Seminar zum Hochschulfernstudium*, Dresden: Zentralstelle für das Hochschulfernstudium des Ministeriums für Hoch- und Fachschulwesens, pp. 14-21.

Guiton, P. (1981) 'Australian distance teaching systems', Paper to conference of Universiti Sains Malaysia, Penang, Malaysia.

Harry, K. (1984) 'The International Centre for Distance Learning's new computerised database', *ICDE Bulletin 6*, 6-7.

Holmberg, B. (1960) *On the Methods of Teaching by Correspondence*, Lund: Gleerup.

Holmberg, B. (1981) *Status and Trends of Distance Education*, London: Kogan Page.

Ilyin, V.V. (1983) 'The USSR Financial and Economic Institute for Education', *Distance Education* 4(2), 142-8.

Karow, W. (1979) *Privater Fernunterricht in der Bundesrepublik Deutschland und in Ausland*, Berlin: DIBB.

Keegan, D. and Rumble, G. (1982) 'Distance teaching at university level', in G. Rumble and K. Harry (eds) *The Distance Teaching Universities*, London: Croom Helm.

Krajnc, A. (1988) 'Social isolation and learning effectiveness in distance education', *ZIFF Papiere 71*, Hagen: Fernuniversität.

Laverty, J. (1980) 'Kevin C. Smith's *External studies at New England*', *Distance Education* 1(2), 207-14.

McKenzie, N., Postgate, R. and Scupham, J. (1975) *Open Learning*, Paris: UNESCO.

Markowitz, H. (1983) 'Independent study by correspondence in American universities', *Distance Education* 4(2), 149-70.

Möhle, H. (1978) *Das in das einheitliche sozialistiche Bildungsswesen der DDR integrierte Hochschulfernstudium*,

Leipzig: Karl-Marx Universität.

Neil, M. (1981) *The Education of Adults at a Distance*, London: Kogan Page.

Ortmeier, A. (1978) *Fernstudium an Universitäten und Fachhochschulen Australiens*, Tübingen: DIFF.

Ortmeier, A. (1981) *Das Fernstudium an den Universitäten und Fachhochschulen Australiens*, Tübingen: DIFF.

Peñalver, A. and Escotet, M. (no date) *Teoria e Praxis de l'Universidad a Distancia*, San Jose: UNED.

Peters, O. (1965) *Der Fernunterricht*, Weinheim: Beltz.

Peters, O. (1971) *Texte zum Hochschulfernstudium*, Weinheim: Beltz.

Rekkedal, T. (1981) *Introducing the Personal Tutor Counsellor in a System of Distance Education*, Stabbek: NKI Norway.

Schramm, W. (1977) *Big Media, Little Media*, London: Sage.

Schwartz, R. (1978) Die Konsultation in Studienprozess des Fernstudiums, in H. Möhle (ed.) *Hoch- und Fachschulfernstudium in der DDR und in entwicklungsländern Afrikas*, Leipzig: KMU.

Sheath, H. (1965) *External Studies at New England: The First Ten Years*, Armidale, NSW: UNE.

Sheath, H. (1973) Report on External Studies, Armidale, NSW: UNE.

Shott, M. (1983a) 'External studies in Australia at the crossroads?', *ASPESA Newsletter* 9(2), 2-9.

Shott, M. (1983b) 'Final report to the ASPESA executive', *ASPESA Newsletter*, 9(3), 15-17.

Singh, B. (1980) *Correspondence education at Indian Universities*, Patiala: Punjabi University.

Smith, K.C. (1979) *External Studies at New England: A Silver Jubilee Review 1955-1979*, Armidale, NSW: UNE.

Smith, K.C. (1984) *Diversity Down Under in Distance Education*, Toowoomba, Queensland: Darling Downs IAE.

TRU report (1975) *An Analysis of Distance Systems*, Stockholm: SOU.

Turnbull, A. (1987) 'Distance education: the trendsetter', *Media in Education and Development* 20(3) 108-12.

Wedemeyer, C. and Bern, H. (1971) 'The independent study division of the University of Wisconsin', in O. Peters, *Texte zum Hochschulfernstudium*, Weinheim: Beltz, pp.29-56.

White, M. (1982) 'A history of external studies in Australia', *Distance Education* 4(2), 101-21.

Willén, B. (1983) 'Distance education in Swedish universities', *Distance Education* 4(2), 211-22.

Zelaya Goodman, C. (no date) 'La administración de los

sistemas de educación a distancia y sus costos, in A. Peñalver, and M. Escotet, *Teoria e Praxis de l'Universidad a Distancia*, San Jose: UNED 1, 141-57.

Chapter Nine

PLANNING DISTANCE SYSTEMS

> The motion picture is the great educator of the poorer
> people. It incites their imagination by bringing the whole
> world before their eyes. It sets spectators thinking and
> raises their standard of living. Books will soon be obsolete
> in the public schools. Scholars will be instructed through
> the eye. It is possible to teach every branch of human
> knowledge with the motion picture. Our school system will
> be completely changed inside of ten years.
>
> Thomas A. Edison, 1913

The typology developed in the previous chapter gives a basis
for planning for distance education. Each of the five models
identified has a theoretical framework and numerous examples
in the world of distance education today.

AN AUTONOMOUS INSTITUTION OR A SUBSECTION OF A CONVENTIONAL ONE?

The first question to be addressed by administrators or
education planners is whether to choose an autonomous
distance institution or a distance subsection of an existing
school, college, or university. Sewart (1986) addresses this
question in an article 'Single mode versus dual mode: a fair
question?'. His conclusion is that distance systems now in
existence are single mode or dual mode because of historical
accident and external factors rather than as a result of
educational debate (1986:15).

In *The Distance Teaching Universities* (1982:245) Keegan
and Rumble initiated the educational debate and proposed
planning guidelines which I believe are still valid. In general
terms the conclusion of that study was that in systems where
there are less than 10,000 enrolments per year one is naturally
inclined towards a department of an existing institution; but

that beyond 20,000 enrolments a distance teaching school, college, or university is the favoured solution.

The final decision for educational planners will depend on a detailed theoretical knowledge of distance education; costs (see Chapter 10); and a detailed knowledge of the social, political, historical, and educational structures of the region in question.

AN AUTONOMOUS INSTITUTION

Large distance institutions like the Centre National d'Enseignement à Distance in France with 250,000 students from 107 countries in 1988 or Sukkhothai Thammatirat Open University in Bangkok with 450,000 students in 1988 have no need for conventional face-to-face students. Where would they put them? Their whole cost structures are built on the premise that they do not have to build buildings for students.

In the same way the full-time staff of such institutions are fully occupied in designing floppy disks, video, audio, and printed materials for future students together with the teaching at a distance of students presently enrolled in courses previously developed. One cannot realistically expect such staff to take on in addition a third major area of didactic activity: lecturing in lecture halls and providing tutorials for face-to-face students.

If the choice is in favour of a separate distance institution then one has to consider the advantages of the correspondence school model (Group 1) or the distance teaching university model (Group 2) or a multi-level structure.

Group 1 models

Most proprietary institutions are Group 1 models (Glatter and Wedell 1971; Weinstock 1976; Karow 1979). Some are quite small, well below the 10,000 enrolments recommended by Rumble and Keegan, but have existed happily for decades.

Some Group 1 government institutions in Australia, Canada, and New Zealand have less than 10,000 enrolments but have survived successfully for 60-70 years. Some are quite large: the New South Wales College of External Studies had 30,000 students in 1986 (Erdos 1986), the Technical Correspondence School at Lower Hutt had 40,000 (Ostman and Wagner 1987) and the Alberta Correspondence School 50,000 (Turnbull 1987).

Group 2 models: the distance teaching universities

Dodd and Rumble (1984) have analysed the planning process when the choice falls on a distance teaching university. In a study that ranges widely from Nigeria to Costa Rica and Japan they leave the impression that the personal view of particular politicians played a decisive role in the period from the Report of the National Planning Committee (a stage in most developments in the study) to the creation or abandonment of the project.

Most of the open universities studied in the 1982 book *The Distance Teaching Universities* quickly reached the 10,000 volume suggested by Rumble and Keegan. Some, like the Asian foundations of the 1980s, are very large with hundreds of thousands of students. Athabasca University, in Northern Alberta, has had difficulties reaching the suggested size but has survived nevertheless.

Of particular importance to students is the planning of the Open Universeit in the Netherlands (Chang *et al*. 1983). This is a distance teaching university in a country with minimal distances and an excellent network of universities that raced to 50,000 enrolments soon after its inception.

A DEPARTMENT OF AN EXISTING INSTITUTION

There are three basic models if the choice is for a department of an existing institution. These models are normally found in publicly funded institutions at university and college level, rather than proprietary ones. Morrison (1988), nevertheless, forecasts major distance education developments from North American business conglomerates and, if this forecast should prove valid, this might be the model chosen.

Group 3 models: correspondence study departments

Models for analysis abound. Group 3 is a frequent choice for distance education in higher education institutions in the United States of America, Canada, France, Sweden, India and South America.

For the student and the planner the 1983 article by Markowitz 'Independent study by correspondence in American universities' will provide a useful introduction as will a subsequent article by the same author on the costing of such departments (Markowitz 1987).

Group 4: the consultation model

The structure consists of a central materials development agency that brings together teams of professors for course development from a selection of the colleges and universities in the state or nation. The central institution provides the permanent team of experts in instructional design and realization.

The materials developed are then distributed to all the colleges or universities within the system from which students are to be taught and consultations organized.

Such a system works best in carefully planned, centrally controlled education systems like that of the German Democratic Republic. Adaptations of the model, nevertheless, are of interest to students and planners elsewhere.

Group 5: the New England model

Among the options available when the choice is for a department of an existing school, college, or university is the Group 5 structure sometimes referred to as the New England model or the Australian integrated mode.

The fundamental difference between Group 5 structures and those of Groups 3 and 4 is the changes that the distance department occasions in the structure of the rest of the university. Staffing workloads, departmental priorities, and costings are modified in this model to enable full-time faculty to teach both on-campus and off-campus students. Whether planners can consider a Group 5 structure will depend on university legislation and tradition in their state or nation.

OTHER SOLUTIONS

In certain circumstances none of the five major models may work. The planning of a distance university system for Italy in 1983 was confronted by the impossibility of the Parliament legislating for a distance university (Group 2) and by the problem that centuries of Italian university legislation made Groups 3-5 quite untenable.

The solution found was a consortium. Basically this was a business structure which paid leading academics to write distance learning materials as if they were writing a book. Students enrolled in one of the universities which joined the consortium. The consortium organized student support services and paid tutors but the students returned to the universities for the examinations as conventional students (Keegan and Lata 1985).

STUDENTS

Detailed analyses of distance students have been published by many institutions. Planners of distance systems will be concerned with the characteristics of distance students and the retention of students in the system.

Characteristics

A major grouping of students who have chosen to study at a distance is the enrolment of the Open University of the UK. A detailed analysis of these students undertaken by Field (1982) identifies four characteristics which differentiate these students from the traditional university undergraduate in Britain: experience, aspirations, study milieu, and investment.

The major findings of Field's analysis of OUUK students and university students in general might be presented as in Table 9.1. In general distance students tend to be gainfully employed, have less prior education, are older, and live comparatively far away from the nearest place offering the same course in a different form.

Privatization of the study process and isolation from teacher and peer group remain the central distinctive features of distance students. These are factors that make studying at a distance a perilous task for those who cannot benefit from privacy.

Drop-outs

Preoccupation about drop-outs is a constant feature of distance education literature and practice, though *not* at primary and secondary school level. A possible theoretical basis for an analysis of drop-out in distance education might be an adaptation of Tinto's work on drop-out in on-campus courses to the problem of studying at a distance. Tinto developed a theoretical model, based ultimately on Durkheim, in which it was hypothesized that weakness of integration of the student into the social fabric of the institution was an indicator of possible drop-out (Sweet 1986).

Table 9.1 Differences between OUUK students and other university students

Students generally	OU students
1. Experience	
People under 25, with little direct experience of employment; of the application of knowledge or techniques in service or industrial settings; of human relations or of social changes	75 per cent aged 30-55 with a diverse accumulation of experience; with ideas on evidence, accuracy and analysis not gained from schooling. For many learning starts with un-learning
2. Aspirations	
People locked into education because of selection and training; because of family expectations; because of tied income and for whom in the current economic climate there is no attractive alternative	For some, university studies are central as there is no other way to fulfil aspirations; or study gives a new dimension to existing work; or study is marginal with family and job responsibilities dominating it
3. Study milieu	
Easy access to learning media; to fellow students; to advisers and tutors; leisure facilities are complementary to study; all within a convenient distance	The study milieu is generally characterized by its distance from the source of instruction; the distance in time caused by the mismatch between student-system time and institutional time
4. Investment	
Traditionally a paid-for place in an institution of higher education has been the surest route to a clean, pleasant and interesting job. More recently it is a postponing of unemployment or work experience. Graduates emerge not very useful immediately to employers but they can be developed and exploited by employers	The student takes on and finds money for an extra workload, a departure from most of his peers. To the family of the student the return may be less tangible than from other activities. The graduates are older, expensive and less mobile but with extensive experience of life

Source: Adapted from Field (1982).

If one were to accept this theory, virtually all distance students would be 'at risk'. Their integration into the structure of their university or college is fragile and continually so throughout the length of the study programme. The distance student, almost by definition, does not take part in the life of the institution and the industrialization of distance systems works to produce a customer/business atmosphere which negates the integrative support mechanisms which Tinto hypothesizes as vital. The privatization of learning at a distance tends further to provoke lack of integration.

This study suggests that there is a propensity to dropout by enrollees in distance education. This propensity can be attenuated by the planning of quality learning materials but above all by the provision of adequate student support services for the avoidance of avoidable drop-out. Where student support of an adequate nature is not provided, students should understand that distance study may be constantly fraught with the risk of discontinuation.

Time

Time available for study is closely related to success or failure in distance education; it is also closely related to drop-out. The German scholar Schwittmann, studied the relation between time available for study and success at both the Funkkolleg programmes by radio in Southern Germany and the courses at the Fernuniversität in North-Rhine Westfalen.

Schwittmann (1982) claims that 'time available for study' is the only important variable for predicting success or failure in a distance study programme. He goes further and forecasts that from a multi-media study package (including visits to study centres, watching television programmes, listening to radio programmes, studying course materials, doing assignments) one can forecast which element of the multimedia study package will be dropped first when one knows the relevance of each element towards the final examination and the amount of time available to the student.

COURSES

Holmberg (1981:14,49) has shown that most subject areas can be taught at a distance, whether in terms of Bloom's taxonomy or of the learning styles of Marton and Säljö.

Questions for planners arise concerning the status and accreditation of the courses chosen. Study at a distance is arduous (Chapter 4). The status of learning at a distance is fragile (Chapter 7). There is little purpose in studying at a distance for years to gain a degree or a diploma if you then find that the degree or diploma is not valid for further study or has little status with managers at employment interviews.

Status for distance awards depends in large measure on the acceptance of the theoretical basis for distance education by faculty members of university education departments and on the acceptance by vice-chancellors and senior administrators of conventional institutions of the validity of qualifications won at a distance.

Accreditation

The quality of distance courses and their accreditation contribute to the status of distance courses.

A national system of accreditation of degrees and diplomas at all levels, as in France, works in favour of a distance system. Such a system is, however, often criticized as lacking in freedom and flexibility. It works, none the less, in favour of the distance system as there is instant status and national accreditation for the study at a distance.

Similarly in Italian universities examinations are oral, and this system can cause problems for commentators from other backgrounds. It seems, none the less, quite appropriate that students who have studied for university qualifications at a distance should be examined face-to-face.

Group 1 government-sponsored institutions are usually accredited as the distance component of nationwide systems. Group 1 privately supported institutions are usually monitored by national associations like the NHSC in the United States of America and the Association of European Correspondence Schools, both of which have gained in stature in recent decades.

Group 2 institutions, like other universities, have accreditation built into their charters. Some, in addition, appoint external examiners.

Group 3 institutions participate in the university or college accreditation of their respective countries, though some distance departments have difficulty in winning accreditation for the award of whole degrees at a distance, especially at post-graduate level.

Group 4 and 5 institutions usually have little trouble with

accreditation as they participate in the award structure of their college or university, with students sitting for the same assessment procedures as on-campus students in the same courses.

CHOICE OF MEDIUM

Literature

This is the area of the field of distance education which has been most widely researched and on which the volume of publication is rapidly increasing. Whitehead (1988) has provided students with bibliographies to the most important volume of this research, that of the Institute of Educational Technology of the OUUK, and authorative overviews and analyses have been published by Bates (1980, 1981, 1982, 1984, 1988).

History

Distance systems have dealt with the use of media in education for over 100 years but the evidence for the whole of this period has not been subjected to analysis. There have been frequent forecasts, like that of Edison in 1913 about the cinematograph, that one medium would come to dominate either on-campus or off-campus.

Context

Planners of distance systems approach the choice of media with decisions to be made on quantity of education (the avoidance of avoidable drop-out), quality, and status of education and costs. Commentators in the late 1980s called for choice of media to be linked to context and this is always important for distance systems. Boyd from Concordia University writes of 'The impact of society on educational technology' and concludes that 'the cyclic swings of societal norms and the ineluctable momentum of our heavy econo-political machinery squeeze and twist our technical options in education to a frustrating, sometimes even to a disastrous degree' (1988:121).

What medium then should be chosen? It often comes as a surprise to those who do not know distance system that there are two answers to that question. The choice of media to carry the content of the course may be quite different from the media chosen for the presentation of the course to students. Print may be a good choice of medium for the content of many courses (Landry 1985), but when the course is in presentation students may need rapid feedback by telephone, electronic mail, computer-, or teleconferencing (Holmberg 1984:50).

Many scholars (Ruggles *et al.* 1982) have provided listings of the excellent range of technologies now available to the planners of distance systems.

ADMINISTRATION

Miller and Rice (1967) in their *Systems of Organisation. The Control of Task and Sentient Boundaries*, show how organizations can be characterized by their essential operating activities and show the importance of analysing task boundaries and sentient (personal) boundaries in administration. In Miller and Rice's terms it is important to identify the 'operating activities' that characterize the enterprise. The operating activities are those that directly contribute to the import/conversion/export processes which define the nature of the enterprise and differentiate it from other enterprises.

Miller and Rice's theory of system organization was applied to the organization of distance education systems by Kaye and Rumble (1981). They had little difficulty in identifying two characteristic operating subsystems 'course development' and 'student support services' and the task boundaries that separate these activities within the organization from other activities (see Fig. 9.1). The *course development subsystem* comprises the planning, designing, crystallizing, and recording of the teaching (together with the proposed methodologies and structures for presenting the teaching at a future date) in mechanical or electronic form. The *student support subsystem* comprises the activities designed by the institution to focus on the student's home (or institutional centre near the student's home) that will provide a private and individualized presentation of the pre-recorded course content together with the simulation of teacher and peer-group clarification, that normally accompany the presentation of courses in oral, group-based educational provision.

Figure 9.1 Administrative subsystems in a distance education system

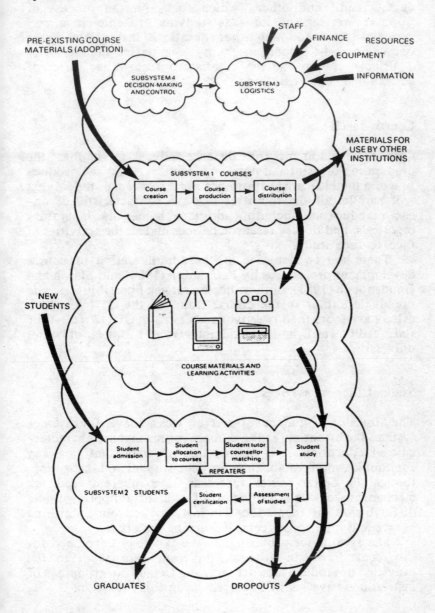

Source: Reproduced with permission from Kaye and Rumble (1981)

Distance education enterprises have clusters of task and sentient boundaries which focus on the process of 'course development' and others which focus on the process of 'support services for students studying at home' in a way which cannot be found in other educational institutions. These two characteristic operating subsystems define the nature of a distance system and differentiate it from other forms of educational administration.

Course development

Course development for distance education implies the preparation of print and non-print materials plus the production of a total learning experience for the distance student that will parallel all the facilities that are characteristic of on-campus education, including additional homework, laboratory practicals, and library research periods and all the activities of face-to-face study.

There are two studies of the administration of course development procedures by K.C. Smith (1980) and Mason and Goodenough (1981). Both indicate a range of possibilities from the single author to the course teams of the OUUK which often have more than twenty members from OUUK full-time staff, BBC staff and consultants from business or other universities.

Student support services

The provision of student support services achieves for distance systems the essential feedback mechanisms that are characteristic of education. It is mainly through them that two-way communication is established between student and institution, though the better course materials have inherent feedback mechanisms as well. Provision of student support services distinguishes distance education institutions from publishing houses and other producers of learning materials.

The five major groupings in the typology developed for this book have, in general, different approaches to the provision of student support services. Two of the groupings of institutions have heavy involvement in this provision:

- Group 4: the consultation system of the central and Eastern European socialist democracies; and
- Group 5: the Australian integrated mode.

Two groupings of institutions have tended to rely on the development of learning materials as central, with student support focusing on attentive correction and comment on assignments:

* Group 1: the correspondence schools and colleges; and
* Group 3: the independent study model.

The fifth grouping (Group 2, the autonomous distance teaching universities) varies widely in theoretical and financial commitment to student support services.

PLANNING FOR THE FUTURE

In the distance education university of the 1990s the lecturer sits all day long at his or her wordprocessor. The content of the course is input into the wordprocessor and the lecturer prints out a hard copy from the printer. No secretary or typing pool support is used and the need to proofread for other person's errors is eliminated. The lecturer corrects the hard copy, puts in the corrections and prints out a final version of the course materials to ensure that the text is correct. He or she then inserts the university's house style instructions for headings, subdivisions, choice of type-face, and layout.

The lecturer then turns to his or her mouse to prepare the computer-designed illustrations, graphs, diagrams, and other illustrative features that he or she wishes to use as part of the teaching. When these are completed to the lecturer's satisfaction, they are blended electronically into the text. The text and illustrations are printed out and the printed materials for the course are now complete.

The materials can be distributed to the students' computers by satellite and the student can decide whether to study them on screen or print a hard copy. Alternatively the materials can be photocopied or plates can be made for conventional printing. The whole process of teaching at a distance has been industrialized and rationalized with the elimination of inter-mediary persons between the lecturer and the students.

As the lecturer spends much of his or her time at the wordprocessor or in the audio, video, or computer design laboratory when not working at the wordprocessor, the teaching style of the distance education lecturer has evolved far from that of the on-campus university and the skills and training required are quite different. The lecturer needs the skills of a wordprocessor operator, of an instructional designer, graphic artist, and layout expert for print materials and extensive skills in the development and evaluation of audio, video, and computer-based materials.

Side by side with the electronic developments in the work of the distance educator of the 1990s come developments in what has been called by Rumble (1987) 'the information technology university'. Rumble foresees the computerized integration of the main systems of a distance teaching university (materials design, production of physical materials, student services, tuition and assessment, administrative services) into one information technology network.

REFERENCES

Bates, A. (1980) 'Towards a better theoretical framework for the use of audio-visual media', *Instructional Science*, **10**, 41-55.

Bates, A. (1981) 'The unique educational characteristics of TV and some consequences for teaching and learning', *Journal of Educational Television*, 141-9.

Bates, A. (1982) 'Trends in the use of audio-visual media', in J. Daniel *et al. Learning at a Distance. A World Perspective*. Edmonton: ICCE.

Bates, A. (1984) *Broadcasting in Education: An Evaluation*, London: Constable.

Bates, A. (1988) 'Technology and distance education in Canada', in *Proceedings of Distance Education Symposium*, Lakehead University, Thunder Bay, 24-26 March.

Boyd, G. (1988) 'The impact of society on educational technology', *British Journal of Educational Technology* 19(2), 114-22.

Carr, R. (1984) 'Course development procedures', *ICDE Bulletin*, **5**, 21-7.

Chang, T. *et al.*, (1983) *Distance learning. On the Design of an Open University*, Boston: Kluwer-Nijhoff.

Dodd, J. and Rumble, G. (1984) 'Planning new distance teaching universities', *Higher Education* 13(3), 171-97.

Edison, Thomas Alva (1913) 'The evolution of the motion picture (interview with Frederick James Smith)', *The New York Dramatic Mirror*, 9 July, 24-5.

Erdos, R. (1986) *Some Developments in Distance Education in Australia*, Hagen: Fernuniversität (ZIFF).

Field, J. (1982) 'Characteristics of OU students', *Teaching at a Distance Research Supplement* No. 1. Milton Keynes: OU.

Glatter, R. and Wedell, E. (1971) *Study by Correspondence*, London: Longman.

Holmberg, B. (1981) *Status and Trends in Distance Education*, London: Kogan Page.

Holmberg, B. (1984) 'On the educational potentials of information technology with special regard to distance education', *ICDE Bulletin* 6, 49-54.

Karow, W. (1979) *Privater Fernunterricht in der BDR und in Ausland*, Berlin: BIBB.

Kaye, A. and Rumble, G. (1981) *Distance Teaching for Higher and Adult Education*, London: Croom Helm.

Keegan, D. and Lata, F. (1985) *L'Università a Distanza*, Milan: Angeli.

Keegan, D. and Rumble, G. (1982) 'The distance teaching universities: an appraisal', in G. Rumble and K. Harry (eds) *The Distance Teaching Universities*, London: Croom Helm.

Landry, F. (1985) 'L'imprimé: un moyen d'enseignement privilégié', in F. Henri and A. Kaye *Le Savoir à Domicile*, Québec: Téléuniversité, pp.209-59.

Markowitz, H. (1983) 'Independent study by correspondence in American universities', *Distance Education* 4(2), 149-70.

Markowtiz, H. (1987) 'Financial decision making - calculating the costs of distance education', *Distance Education* 8(2), 147-60.

Mason, J. and Goodenough, S. (1981) 'Course development', in A. Kaye and G. Rumble, *Distance Teaching for Higher and Adult Education*, London: Croom Helm.

Miller, E. and Rice, A. (1967) *Systems of Organisation. The Control of Task and Sentient Boundaries*, London: Tavistock.

Morrison, T. (1988) 'Policy technology and globalism. Charting the future of distance education', in *Proceedings of Distance Education Symposium*, Lakehead University, Thunder Bay, 24-26 March.

Ostman, R. and Wagner, G. (1987) 'New Zealand management students' perceptions of communications technology in correspondence education', *Distance Education* 8(1), 47-60.

Ruggles, R. *et al.* (1982) *Learning at a Distance and the New Technology*, Vancouver: ERICB.

Rumble, G. (1987) 'Why distance teaching can be cheaper than conventional education', *Distance Education* 8(1), 72-94.

Schwittman, D. (1982) 'Time and learning in distance education', *Distance Education* 3(1), 155-71.

Sewart, D. (1978) *Continuity of Concern for Adults Studying at a Distance*, Hagen: Fernuniversität (ZIFF).

Sewart, D. (1986) 'Single mode versus dual model: a fair question?', *Open Campus* 12, 10-15.

Smith, K.C. (1980) 'Course development procedures', *Distance Education* 1(1), 61-7.

Smith, P. and Kelly, M. (1987) *Distance Education and the Mainstream*, London: Croom Helm.

Sweet, R. (1986) 'Student drop-out in distance education: an application of Tinto's model', *Distance Education* 8(2), 201-19.

Turnbull, A. (1987) 'Distance education: the trendsetter', *Media in Education and Development* 20(3), 108-12.

Weinstock, N. (1976) *Les Cours par Correspondance du Secteur Privé en Belgique*, Brussels: Centre National de Sociologie du Droit Civil.

Whitehead, R. (1988) *The Institute Bibliography*, Milton Keynes: OUUK (IET) microfilm.

Part IV

EVALUATION

Chapter Ten

ECONOMICS

'Put yourself in my place,' said the Minister. 'You're asking me to make a tough decision, but you're not giving me the facts.'

The Secretary for Education shuffled through his papers, as if he might find the answers there, like a joker in a pack of cards.

'You see, sir, we aren't sure how much this technology will cost in real terms, but we hope it will be less than we'd have to spend providing the same education by other means.'

'You really expect me to believe that these new machines can teach just as well as my teachers? Where's your proof? What's happened in other countries?'

'Well, sir, we certainly don't know much yet about what children learn this way, but there's a similar project starting in Bothana in 1980'.

The Minister frowned and said, in a snarling tone, 'So, we don't know what it costs and we don't know whether it works, but you still expect me to risk my political reputation on it. What's the alternative?'

'More and more children not being educated sir,' the Secretary said quietly.

'Why's that?'

'We can't afford the usual education any more, sir. We simply must try to increase our cost-effectiveness by using technology.'

'But can technology increase the cost-effectiveness of education?'

'There's some doubt if you will ever know whether technology can increase education's cost-effectiveness,' interjected the Professor, unable to restrain himself any longer.

Across the table, the Minister looked even more

161

annoyed. He really needed an answer.

'We haven't had great success in judging cost-effectiveness in education,' the Professor went on, puffing on his pipe. 'Many of the assumptions underlying this type of analysis simply don't apply in the field of education. You can't treat education as an industry, for example'.

'But surely the chances of carrying out this analysis are increased when technology is introduced on a grand scale?', asked the Secretary.

'Well, the problems lie in identifying costs and effects and then in measuring them. We're getting better at it, but it isn't easy.'

'My members want to know how this new technology will improve their working conditions. They want the money to be spent on employing more teachers, to reduce class sizes. That would be the best way to increase their cost-effectiveness,' claimed the President of the Union of Teachers.

'Hmmm,' said the Minister, 'if we can't measure the cost-effectiveness of technology, we'll have even less chance of measuring the cost-effectiveness of that strategy.'

'You see what I mean', the President trumpeted, 'if you can't tell how cost-effective the teachers are, how can you compare them with the new educational media?'

Jean-Claude Eicher *et al*. 1982

PRE-1970s

Prior to 1970 the economics of distance teaching at university level in the west revolved mainly around the distance/external/independent study departments of conventional universities. In the main, these departments were funded, as was conventional education, by government Ministries of Education from public monies, though the weighting for an external student was normally lower than that of an on-campus student.

In many American universities, distance departments (even when students were studying for college credit) were grouped with continuing education departments and had to be self-supporting. Much of the rest of the world of distance education was proprietary in the early 1970s, if one excepts the correspondence schools and colleges of external studies run by the Australian state and Canadian provincial departments of education and the French CNTE (now CNED).

Prior to 1970 the cost equation for some proprietary

distance education institutions seemed to be based on producing learning materials as cheaply as possible and then enrolling as many students as possible. There was little protective legislation at this period and the national accrediting agencies were not as influential as they were later to become.

Figure 10.1 Contrasting cost structures of proprietary distance systems

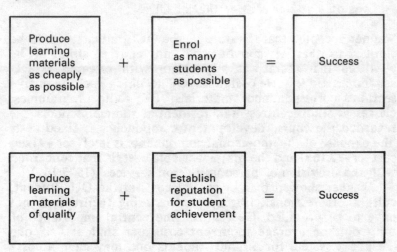

There were many excellent proprietary institutions in the 1970s and earlier - one thinks especially of the members of the National Home Study Council of the USA, the European Home Study Council and the British Association of Correspondence Colleges and similar accrediting associations. For these an analysis would combine the production of learning materials of quality with the costs of ensuring success for students enrolled (see Fig. 10.1)

THE ECONOMICS OF THE OPEN UNIVERSITY (UK)

Cost analyses of the OUUK 1

Wagner (1972) provided the first cost analysis of a distance system with the entry of the OUUK into the field of distance education. He applied the cost structures of conventional universities (CU), taken largely from the Robbins Report, to the budgetary data of the OUUK. The results were impressively in favour of the OU:

- the average recurrent cost per equivalent undergraduate at the OU was only 25 per cent of that of CUs;
- the capital cost per student place at the OU was only 6 per cent of the conventional figure;
- the average recurrent cost per graduate - which depends on drop-outs - would be in favour of the OU unless its drop-out rate went over 85 per cent; and
- the resource cost per equivalent undergraduate at the OU was only 16 per cent of that of CUs.

Wagner accepted that the output, the OU graduate, would be similar to that of conventional universities although he admitted that there was a problem with research as OU academics did less. He costed the OU teaching package in five sections: correspondence materials, TV, radio programmes, classes at study centres, and residential summer schools. He regarded the course development components as fixed costs 'the expense of the impersonal components is in effect a fixed cost' (1972:165) and the major variable cost 'is that concerned with the provision of personal tuition services' (1972:167).

Wagner showed that in capital costs at the OU, student, cultural, recreational, library, and catering facilities do not have to be provided. He realized the central importance of drop-outs on average recurrent costs per student - if one designs a system for 50,000 students one may have a cost-effective system; however, if most drop out, one has a very costly system. However, even in 1972 Wagner refused to accept traditional drop-out statistics for correspondence schools as relevant to his cost structure for the OU. 'The OU is an innovation,' he wrote. 'The OU is much more than a correspondence college, since it offers an integrated system of teaching in which TV, radio, personal tuition and correspondence all play a part' (1972:177).

Carter (1973) objected strongly, stating that a university exists to provide an educational experience, not just to turn out equivalent graduates and that Wagner was costing two quite different kinds of educational experience (1973:69). Wagner had not costed CU faculties like medicine, nor was his allowance for research at CUs adequate. OU courses were all low-level; much of the costs of CUs were for laboratories for post-graduate students.

Carter also claimed that Wagner had forgotten to cost all the services that CUs were doing for the OU (residential schools, study centres, and libraries, etc.).

Wagner replied by recalculating his costs to include science and making adjustments for research, but did not accept most of Carter's other claims. The revised costings came out with little difference from his previous analysis because, Wagner said, Carter was confusing consumption and investment benefits (1973b:72). In Wagner's view although the 'educational experience' of the OU and the CUs was different, the social benefit to the community as measured by future earnings of OU graduates would be the same.

In a 1973 paper in *Universities Quarterly* Wagner re-presented his arguments in the context of a national goal of expanding the 15 per cent of each age cohort who entered higher education in the UK in 1971. He suggested the substitution of capital for labour by increasing the role of impersonal tuition by means of correspondence and broadcasting at the OU since 'educational technology remains at CUs a *complement* to existing methods of tuition instead of a *substitute*' (1973a:404).

Wagner now admitted the validity of more of Carter's claims and re-presented his figures in slightly modified form. His general conclusion of the cost effectiveness of the OU was unchanged. 'Academic salaries', he states, 'which are the main item in costs at a conventional university take up less than 15% of OUUK costs and are unrelated to student numbers' (1973a:398). He also pointed out that the OUUK system was devised for its educational effectiveness as a distance teaching system, not because it was cheap (1973a:400). Various ways of making it cheaper are considered: reducing personal tuition and increasing correspondence being the basic ones.

Cost analyses of the OUUK 2

Laidlaw and Layard (1974) moved the analysis from the cost of the OUUK to the costs of courses at the OUUK, seeking to throw light on the costs of OU teaching methods as against conventional 'live' instruction.

They distinguish between four 'types of cost' at the OU (1974:445):

1. *fixed course costs:* inescapable if the course is put on;
2. *variable course costs:* costs which are dependent on student volume;
3. *fixed central costs:* inescapable if the OU is to exist; and
4. *variable central university costs:* which alter with the volume of students.

They conclude, like Wagner, that the real strength of the OU system is (1974:452) 'the potential economies of scale which can be reaped by substituting capital for labour'.

This means that a major part of the costs of the course become fixed and invariant with respect to student numbers. By contrast, campus universities' courses have low fixed costs but high marginal costs. For low levels of operation the campus university is the more efficient system and for high levels the OU is.

The breakeven point in 1971 was calculated at 21,691 students, at which point the OUUK average cost per student would be lower than that for CUs.

Cost analyses of the OUUK 3

In 1975 Lumsden and Ritchie presented a survey and cost analysis of the OUUK. Their argument tends to support the position taken up by both Wagner and Laidlaw/Layard. In particular they attempt to answer the question 'What is the contribution towards the final degree of an average student year in the OU compared to an average student year in a conventional university?' and provide four different sets of answers. The article speaks of 'mass-media lectures' (1975:238) on radio and television as central to the system and concludes with a discussion of the costing of a television university in the US.

Cost analyses of the OUUK 4

In 1977 Wagner returned to the debate with a well-known article 'The economics of the OU revisited'. His appraisal of his forecasts of expenditure in the earlier articles was that they were generally accurate but that the OU had admitted more students than planned so that some costs were, in fact, marginally lower.

In this new study the input is weighted even more heavily in favour of the OU by claiming that costings should not be of graduates, but of what is value-added to produce the graduate. Thus in British CUs one starts with at least two 'A' levels; at the OU one starts normally with much less. No re-evaluation of output (the value of the graduate from OU or CU to employers, the community, or post-graduate research) is, however, considered necessary.

The 1977 article introduces data for forecast and more sophisticated analysis of distance systems. Thus, the drop-out rate of finally enrolled students is set at 25 per cent per course; the costs of course production are rightly assigned to the years before presentation (1977:366); the equation $C = a + bx + y$ where C = fixed costs; x = number of courses; y = number of students, is introduced from Laidlaw and Layard (1974) and Rumble (1976). A new distinction is made between new course production and maintenance of existing courses.

There are two major conclusions from Wagner's 1977 study: first, most of the economies of scale of the OU had been reaped within the first few years and there was little hope of further reductions. This was because the economies of increasing student numbers had been used by the OU to increase the number of courses in development and on offer rather than to reach the steady state, and because it proved impossible to improve academic productivity, especially for full-time tenured staff once the institutional patterns had gelled. Second, his analysis can offer little guidance on policy changes within the OU or on the planning of other distance systems.

It is a little disappointing that Wagner offers no comparisons with other systems nor with variants on the OU system. Some suggestions are made (1977:371), however, on reducing face-to-face tutoring, reducing summer school attendance, lowering the quality of printing or layout of materials - the normal suggestions that distance systems face when they need to cut costs. Wagner claims that all of these would change the nature of the product the OU offers to students.

Carnoy and Levin (1975) and Mace (1978) were the first to challenge these conclusions. Carnoy and Levin claim that:

> The limited nature of Open University education as well as the credential effect of particular institutions on earnings and occupational attainments would suggest that the Open University graduate is not likely to receive either consumption or income benefits from his education that are as high as those of the person from the more conventional university setting.
>
> (Carnoy and Levin 1975:231)

Mace considered that the claim of the OU to be more cost effective than CUs was not substantiated. His OU article challenged both the economic analysis of Wagner and the 'openness' of the OU as it had been presented in a number of articles, especially by McIntosh (1976).

Mace's position is clear:

It is concluded after an examination of the methodology
and the evidence, that neither the economic case nor the
social case is substantiated. Moreover, this view of the
OU's performance may constitute a dangerous myth,
because it may well inhibit further attempts at economic
evaluation of the OU.

(Mace 1978:295)

Mace bases much of his criticism of Wagner on the evaluation
of the output of the OU system: earnings forgone, competit-
iveness on the labour market, and the value-added by the OU.
He accepts Wagner's costing that it takes one-half of CU costs
to produce a graduate at the OU and one-third of CU costs
for the average recurrent annual cost per student, but asks
whether the measure of output (graduates), could be produced
more cheaply by reducing or reallocating resources between
the various items in the OU budget (1978:305).

The answer is that it could but that you produce a
different teaching package and this alters the quality and
possibly the quantity of the output. Mace's main candidates
for reduction are television broadcasting and class tutorials
which, he suggests, could be reduced without affecting the
quantity, quality, and status of the output.

COST ANALYSES OF DISTANCE SYSTEMS

The economics of distance systems takes on a new dimension
with the chapter by Neil *et al.* in the 1979 book *Fernstudien
an Universitäten* edited by Dörfler and published in Vienna. It
is clear from the opening sentence that the parochialism of the
Wagner-Mace debate has been left behind:

In numerous instances, we have observed the launching
of distance learning systems for which the fundamental
variables which affect costs to a significant extent have
either not been made explicit or have not been given
explicit working values in initial budgeting exercises.

(Neil *et al.* 1979:3)

Valuable as the economic analyses of the OU had been,
they had not extrapolated from the context of a single
institution which has been described as *sui generis* (Daniel and
Stroud 1981:148) and which offers an unusual, if highly
successful, costing mix of extensive television broadcasting
with large amounts of compulsory and optional face-to-face

sessions - a costing structure characteristic of none of the five models in this book's typology, not even Group 2: the distance teaching universities.

Neil *et al.* base themselves on the economic analyses of distance teaching systems outlined above *plus* the work done on the economic analysis of media in education during the 1970s by Eicher, Jamison, Klees, Wells, and others. As a result they seek to provide costing processes that will be of value to all workers in distance systems.

They express the cost functions so far established as:

$$TC = F + VN$$

where TC = total costs; F = fixed costs; V = variable cost per unit of output (N); and N = number of units of output (students/student hours, etc.). When the total cost function is linear, the average cost (AC) is simply equal to the fixed cost dividend by N plus the variable cost (V), so that AC = F/N + V and the marginal cost is equal to V.

They confirm the findings of previous studies, especially those of Laidlaw and Layard:

- The cost structures of distance learning systems differ significantly from those of traditional instructional systems (1979:98).
- Distance systems have high fixed costs and low variable costs relative to conventional campus-based universities (Laidlaw and Layard, 1974).
- Distance systems have potential for effecting economies of scale: as the number of students increases so the average cost declines by spreading the fixed cost over more units (1979:98).
- For smaller numbers of students, campus-based universities using traditional instructions are more efficient, but for higher numbers a distance system is more efficient (1979:100).
- Design and production costs are generally much higher than the costs of transmission and reception (1979:100).
- There must be sufficient students to allow economies of scale to be reaped (1979:102).

The authors then present their own financial model of a distance system based on three major areas of costing: (i) the organization, (ii) the number of courses, and (iii) the number of students.

This study is important because it transformed what had

Evaluation

been a series of studies of a particular institution into a modelling process for distance systems in general; it used the work of Eicher, Jamison, and others on the costing of educational communications media, and it separated clearly the analysis of cost-inducing variables in distance education systems from the economics of conventional institutions.

CANADIAN SMALL DISTANCE EDUCATION SYSTEMS

North American financial and management practice was brought into the economics of distance education as a result of studies at Athabasca University, Edmonton, Alberta by Snowden and Daniel. They present (1980:78) a cost equation for small distance education systems based on the two functions of course development and services by delivery:

$$TC = a_1(x_1 + x_2/1) + by + c$$

where

$x_1 =$ course credits 'in development';
$x_2 =$ course credits 'in delivery';
$1 =$ the lifetime of a course in delivery, where it is assumed that the total cost of maintenance over the life of a course is equal to that of developing a course. 1 is taken to be 5 years in practice;
$y =$ weighted course enrolments. Course enrolments are on the basis of a standard 6-credit course, such that a student enrolled on a 3-credit course is equal to 0.5 of a standard course enrolment;
$a_1 =$ course development costs per credit;
$b =$ delivery costs per weighted course enrolment; and
$c =$ costs of institutional overheads.

This model differentiates costs for courses in development which will be taught in the future from courses already developed which are now being taught.

Snowden and Daniel show the average recurrent cost per course enrolment declines as the number of course enrolments increases, but at a declining rate, so that once a small distance education system reaches about 10,000 course enrolments, with a media mix and student support services similar to those of Athabasca University, then further economies of scale cannot be expected to be important.

COSTING OF EDUCATIONAL TECHNOLOGY

The economics of new educational media have been studied by a number of leading experts in the field of the use of new communications technology in education: J.C. Eicher, D.T. Jamison, S. Klees, E. McAnany, J. Mayo, F. Orivel, H. Perraton, and P. Suppes. Schramm's 1977 overview *Big Media, Little Media* is also well known. These studies have been summarized in a three volume UNESCO study (Eicher *et al.* 1977, 1979, 1982) and a volume edited for the World Bank by Perraton (1982a).

These studies deal with the costing of the use of certain new communications media in education and not with whole distance education systems costs. Many of the programmes which are central to the economic analyses of these studies would not be included in the definition of distance education adopted for this book. For a true costing of such projects one would have to include the school buildings, other plant, and some of the payment to the face-to-face teachers. This would confuse the functional basis for the economics of distance systems.

In 1982 Perraton published *The Cost of Distance Education*, a 65 page summary of the evidence to date analysing the Wagner, Laidlaw-Layard, Snowden-Daniel, Rumble series of studies, together with the work of Eicher, Jamison and the UNESCO/World Bank series, and providing his own synthesis (1982b).

WHOLE DISTANCE EDUCATION SYSTEM COSTS

Rumble had established his cost analysis and financial modelling structures by the late 1970s. In the early 1980s he set about applying his structures to actual situations. This produced two major economic case studies of UNED in Costa Rica (1981:375-401) and of UNA in Venezuela (1982:116-40) and an overview of economics and cost structures which was published as Chapter 12 of *Distance Teaching for Higher and Adult Education* (1981b: 220-34).

In his 1982 article Rumble presented a 'state of the art' analysis of the economics of distance education as it was in 1980. The presentation is so nuanced, qualified, and comprehensive that it is best to present here his conclusions almost in full:

- Broadly speaking, very significant costs are incurred

in the preparation of materials irrespective of student numbers. The level of cost incurred will vary depending on the choice of media. Production costs of television are high but not as high as for film. The production cost of radio is relatively low. Print production costs vary depending on the level of sophistication, but overall are not normally significant in themselves within the context of a particular project. Where print is the principal medium the cost of academic staff time in its design and development may be significant.

- Transmission and duplication costs are very high for video systems. The cost of film and of video-cassette based systems increases with the magnitude of the project. The cost of distributing print and audio-visual materials to students depends on the means of distribution used, population dispersal, and difficulty of access to the target population.

- In conventional educational systems teaching costs are traditionally held to be a recurrent cost that is variable with the number of students in the system. In contrast, in distance learning systems the cost of developing the materials can be regarded as a fixed cost that can be written off over the life of the course of which they form a part. This investment has been seen as analogous to capital investment in business, representing a move away from the labour intensive nature of conventional teaching systems. It follows that the more students there are using the materials, the lower the average cost per student of the materials. Hence at some point, and this depends on the choice of media, a distance teaching system should become cheaper per unit of output than a traditional system.

- The use of face-to-face tuition tends to undermine the cost advantage of distance teaching by re-introducing a cost element that is directly variable with student numbers. As a result, face-to-face contact is usually restricted particularly at the higher levels and has a different function to that found in conventional systems, where it is a major teaching medium.

- From an economic point of view the investment in course materials is not normally warranted where student numbers are small. As a result the choice of courses in distance teaching systems may be restricted, at least in comparison with conventional systems.

- Administrative systems for the control of course

design, production and distribution and for the teaching of students at a distance tend to be more clearly
differentiated from the academic functions than is the
case in conventional systems, as well as being more
complex in themselves. The initial investment in
administrative systems prior to the enrolment of any
students is likely to be significant and on the whole
more costly than is the case in conventional systems.

(Rumble 1982:119-20)

Rumble's work in a number of distance systems enabled him
to identify the main generators of costs in a distance system
and to show how the costs change as key input or output
variables change.

COSTING OF DISTANCE TEACHING UNIVERSITIES

Keegan and Rumble (1982) applied these economic analyses to
the distance teaching universities. Distance teaching universities (DTUs), they conclude, can be cost effective in comparison with conventional universities, but this may not necessar-
ily be the case. The cost advantage of distance teaching
universities can be undermined if (1982:220):

- the investment in media and materials is excessive, relative
  to the number of students in the system;
- the direct student costs (or variable cost per student) is
  above or on a par with those at conventional universities -
  in which case the DTU will *never* achieve economies of
  scale relative to conventional universities;
- the variable cost per student in a DTU is only marginally
  lower than that in a conventional university, since in this
  case the DTU will need proportionally more students if its
  average costs are to drop significantly below that of the
  conventional universities; or
- the DTU cannot attract sufficient students to warrant the
  investment in the development of its materials and systems.

These factors have important implications for the provision of
face-to-face tuition. The more face-to-face tuition is built
into a distance teaching system, the nearer variable student
costs will be to those found in conventional universities.

Yet if one considers that the quality of academic provision
makes an extensive face-to-face element essential in a distance
teaching university, then DTUs with relatively low student

numbers may not be able both to improve the quality of their provision and retain their present level of cost efficiency relative to conventional universities in their country or province.

COSTING OF AUTONOMOUS AND MIXED DISTANCE INSTITUTIONS

In their 1982 study Keegan and Rumble then proceeded with an attempt to compare the cost structures of autonomous distance teaching institutions (Groups 1 and 2) with the distance departments of conventional institutions (Groups 3-5). They came up with the following cost indicators:

- once an annual minimum of enrolments is guaranteed for the distance system some indicators favour the distance system being autonomous;
- the costs associated with establishing an infrastructure for a distance system and the costs of the preparation of initial course materials are such that a mixed system is to be preferred if an annual minimum of enrolments cannot be guaranteed;
- the annual minimum number of enrolments probably lies in the region 9,000-20,000; and
- these financial indicators depend always on the choice of media, the extent of student support services, the number of courses on offer, and the costs of conventional education in the country.

CONCLUSION

From an analysis of all the studies presented in this chapter certain economic indicators on the costing of distance systems can be put together:

- The economics of conventional education is of little value for the cost analysis of distance systems.
- The equation frequently used in conventional education as the basis for system costs

$$\text{Faculty salary expense} = \frac{\text{Weekly student hours x average faculty salary}}{\text{Average class size x average faculty load}}$$

has little relevance in distance education.

- The proportion of fixed costs to total costs in conventional education (schools, colleges, and universities) is small; this is not true of distance systems.
- Distance systems, like industries, have high capital investment in the production of courses; conventional education is labour-intensive.
- The number of drop-outs in the system is crucial; once drop-outs pass 50 per cent and move towards 100 per cent cost effectiveness vanishes.
- If student support services are face-to-face and compulsory, cost structures rapidly return toward those of conventional education. Some authors appear to suggest that academic success or reduction of drop-out may be linked to provision of student services.

Within these caveats it is clear that there is now available a comprehensive costing system for distance education.

APPLICATION

An attempt is now made to apply these conclusions to the costing of a hypothetical distance system.

We know from studies by Wagner and Laidlaw-Layard on the OUUK, by Snowden and Daniel on Athabasca University, and by Rumble on a series of DTUs, that costs of a distance teaching system have the following characteristics:

- high fixed costs
- low variable costs per student
- design and production costs of materials which depend on the choice of media.

We know that the variable costs per student are dependent on the following variables:

- number of local centres
- number of courses in production
- number of students.

In accordance with this analysis it is possible to develop a mathematical cost function for a distance education system.

The cost of the system in any year is:

$$T + Z$$

where T = recurrent costs and Z = fixed costs (plant, buildings), because

$$T = F + L\alpha + D\beta + Cy + Sx$$

where T = total recurrent costs; F = recurrent fixed costs; L = number of local centres; α = average costs of a local centre; D = number of courses in production, β = cost of design and production of a course; C = number of courses in presentation y = average cost of presentation of a course; S = number of students; and x = average cost per student.

Let us hypothesize that there are 6 local centres (L), 13 courses in development (D), 11 courses in presentation (C), and 500 students (S), and that costs are calculated as follows:

Plant and buildings	$850,000
Fixed recurrent costs	$2,031,200
Average cost of a local centre	$26,073
Average cost of producing a course	$12,033
Average cost of presenting a course	$18,454
Average cost per student	$829

In accordance with these data the costs of the system for a full year are:

Fixed costs (Z)=	$850,000
Recurrent costs (T)=	$2,961,719

Recurrent costs are made up of:

F	=		$2,031,200
La =	$26,073 x 6	=	$156,438
Db =	$12,033 x 13	=	$156,429
Cy =	$18,454 x 11	=	$202,984
Sx =	$829 x 500	=	$414,500
		Total	$2,961,719

Thus total system costs (Z+T) are $3,811,719 and total annual costs (T) are $2,961,719.

DIFFERING LEVELS OF ACTIVITY

In addition one can analyse the costs of a system if it has an increased level of activity. For example, let us assume that

there are now:
- 8 local centres
- 60 courses in presentation
- 10 courses that are remade each year or that each course is remade once every 6 years or that 10 courses are produced each year, and
- 500 or 1,000 or 5,000, or 10,000, or 20,000 students.

Then the total cost (T) is:

Fixed	$2,031,200
8 local centres	$208,584
60 courses in presentation	$1,107,240
10 courses in production	$120,330

and there are

500 students	$414,500
1,000 students	$829,000
5,000 students	$4,145,000
10,000 students	$8,290,000
20,000 students	$16,580,000

Therefore total system costs for different student levels are:

Number	*Total costs*	*Average cost per student*
500	$3,881,854	$7,763 p.a.
1,000	$4,296,354	$4,296 p.a.
5,000	$7,612,354	$1,522 p.a.
10,000	$11,757,354	$1,176 p.a.
20,000	$20,047,354	$1,002 p.a.

COMPARATIVE COSTS

Finally, Rumble has provided us with graphs for demonstrating the comparative costs of distance and conventional students.

Assuming that a certain distance system has fixed costs which are three times those of a conventional system, and that its variable costs are one-third of those of a conventional system, then at a certain point the distance system becomes cheaper per capita than the conventional system. Figure 10.2 (Rumble 1981b:222) shows that fixed costs are constant for campus-based and distance learning systems and are always higher for the distance system. Variable costs, on the other hand, start lower for the campus-based system but quickly reach a breakeven point from which stage on, costs are always

Figure 10.2 The cost structure of conventional and distance education systems

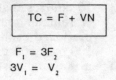

$$TC = F + VN$$

$$F_1 = 3F_2$$
$$3V_1 = V_2$$

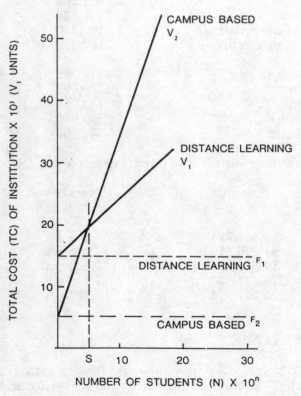

Source: Reproduced with permission from Kaye and Rumble (1981)

When student numbers and unit costs are compared in conventional and distance learning systems (Rumble 1981b:233) as in Fig. 10.3 it is seen that the cost curve quickly favours the distance system but that as student numbers annually increase beyond the 30,000 mark, the curve tends to flatten out and remains permanently parallel to and significantly below the costs of a conventional system.

Figure 10.3 Student numbers and unit costs in conventional and distance systems

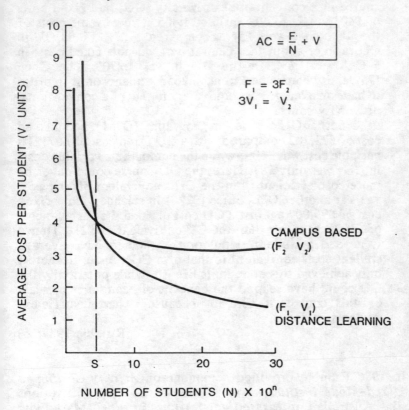

AVERAGE COST PER STUDENT (V_1 UNITS)

$$AC = \frac{F}{N} + V$$

$F_1 = 3F_2$
$3V_1 = V_2$

CAMPUS BASED
(F_2 V_2)

(F_1 V_1)
DISTANCE LEARNING

NUMBER OF STUDENTS (N) X 10^n

Source: Reproduced with permission from Kaye and Rumble (1981)

FURTHER ANALYSES

Rumble addressed the question of when a distance system is more costly than a conventional system and when it can be cheaper in an article published in 1987. Using data from Laidlaw and Layard and from his earlier publications he compared the cost structures of a first year Arts course and a second year Geography course at the Open University of the UK and at a contemporary British university. His conclusions show clearly that some courses at a distance can be cheaper and some can be dearer depending on the cost-inducing variables:

The fixed costs of the first Arts Foundation course offered by the Open University (OU) was £162,558. A comparable course in a conventional university (CU) had fixed costs of £401, a CU to OU ratio of 1:405. The variable costs of the OU course were £56 as compared with £117, an OU to CU ratio of about 1:2. The ratio of variable fixed costs in a CU was 1:3.4. In the OU it was 1:2903. The Open University course had to have 2658 students on it in order to have an average cost equivalent to that of a conventional university course.

Another OU course, on geography (D281), had a fixed cost of £73,702 compared with a CU fixed cost of £671. Its variable cost was £109, while the comparable variable costs in CUs was only £87. Here, the OU course could never be more cost-efficient than the CU's equivalent offerings.

Yet another OU course (S22-) in science, had a fixed cost of £95,007 against a CU cost of £666. Its variable cost of £100 was lower than the CU equivalent of £218. Hence it needed a student population of 800 to have average student costs equivalent to that of a CU course. In fact, it only achieved this once in its life, so, while potentially the OU could have reaped the benefits of economies of scale on this course, it did not because it had insufficient students to do so.

(Rumble 1987:76)

In 1986 Rumble provided a monograph *Activity Costing in Mixed-Mode Institutions* as a guide to Group 5 institutions (the Australian integrated mode) and in 1987 Markowitz published a study of Group 3 institutions (independent study departments) under the title 'Financial decision making – calculating the costs of distance education'.

REFERENCES

Carnoy, M. and Levin, H. (1975) 'Evaluation of educational media: some issues', *Instructional Science* 4, 385-406.

Carter, C.F. (1973) 'The economics of the OU: a comment', *Higher Education* 1, 285-8.

Daniel, J. and Stroud, M. (1981) 'Distance education – a reappraisal for the 1980s', *Distance Education* 2(1), 35-51.

Eicher, J-C. *et al.* (1977, 1980, 1982) *The Economics of New Educational Media*, Paris: UNESCO.

Kaye, A. and Rumble, G. (eds) (1981) *Distance Education for*

Higher and Adult Education, London: Croom Helm.
Keegan, D. and Rumble, G. (1982) 'Characteristics of the distance teaching universities', in G. Rumble and K. Harry (eds) *The Distance Teaching Universities*, London: Croom Helm.
Laidlaw, B. and Layard, R. (1974) 'Traditional versus OU teaching methods: a cost comparison', *Higher Education* 3, 439-68.
Lumsden, K. and Ritchie, C. (1975) 'The Open University: a survey and cost analysis', *Instructional Science* 4, 237-61.
Mace, J. (1978) 'Mythology in the making: is the OU really cost effective?' *Higher Education* 7, 295-309.
Markowitz, H. (1987) 'Financial decision making - calculating the costs of distance education', *Distance Education* 8(2), 147-60.
McIntosh, N. (1976) *A Degree of Difference*, Guildford: SRHE.
Neil, M., Rumble, G. and Tout, A. (1979) 'Some aspects of modelling for recurrent cost budgeting and forecasting in distance learning systems', in W. Dörfert (ed) *Fernstudien an Universitäten*, Klagenfurt: UVD.
Perraton, H. (1982a) *The Cost of Distance Education*, Cambridge: IEC.
Perraton, H. (1982b) *Alternative Routes to Formal Education*, Washington: World Bank.
Rumble, G. (1976) 'Management and costing models for distance teaching', in J. Hakemulder, (ed.) *Distance Education for Development*, Bonn: German Foundation for International Development.
Rumble, G. (1981a) 'The cost analysis of distance teaching: Costa Rica's UNED', *Higher Education* 10, 375-401.
Rumble, G. (1981b) 'Economics and cost structures', in A. Kaye and G. Rumble (eds) *Distance Teaching for Higher and Adult Education*, London: Croom Helm.
Rumble, G. (1982) 'The cost analysis of learning at a distance. Venezuela's UNA', *Distance Education* 4 (2), 101-31.
Rumble, G. (1986) *Activity Costing in Mixed-Mode Institutions*, Geelong: Deakin University.
Rumble, G. (1987) 'Why distance education can be cheaper than conventional education', *Distance Education* 8(1), 72-94.
Schramm, W. (1977) *Big Media, Little Media*, London: Sage.
Snowden, B. and Daniel, J. (1980) 'The economics and management of small, post-secondary distance education systems', *Distance Education* 1(1), 68-91.
Wagner, L. (1972) 'The economics of the Open University',

Higher Education , **2**, 159-83.

Wagner, L. (1973a) 'The OU and the costs of expanding higher education', *Universities Quarterly* 390-410.

Wagner, L. (1973b) 'The economics of the OU: a reply', *Higher Education*, **3**, 21-7.

Wagner, L. (1977) 'The economics of the OU revisted', *Higher Education* **6**, 359-81.

Chapter Eleven

APPRAISAL OF SELECTED SYSTEMS

'I've taught the dog to whistle.'
'I can't hear it whistling.'
'I didn't say it had learned to whistle.'

From a cartoon strip, 1977

In their appraisal of the success or failure of the distance teaching universities (DTUs) Keegan and Rumble (1982) used a four-point evaluation scheme of their effectiveness. This evaluation plan is recommended here as suitable for the overall evaluation of any distance teaching system. Evaluation is focused on:

the quantity of the learning achieved
the quality of the learning achieved
the status of the learning achieved
the relative cost of the learning achieved.

The quantity of the learning achieved

Under this heading are considered:

* the success of the system in widening access, not just in terms of absolute numbers, but in attracting specific target groups;
* drop-outs;
* the quantity of the output relative to the input (the output/input ratio);
* the time it takes to produce the output; and
* the system's success in satisfying national, local and individual needs.

To receive a satisfactory evaluation the institution is required to achieve measurable success in: (i) the avoidance of avoidable drop-out; (ii) the number of successful students as a proportion of the number of students admitted; and (iii) the time it takes for students to achieve successful outcomes.

The quality of learning achieved

Under this heading is grouped the gathering of data for the evaluation of:

- the quality of the learning materials provided by the distance system;
- the extent to which distance teaching is a suitable vehicle for educating students in certain subjects;
- the extent to which education is provided as opposed to instruction;
- the effectiveness of learning at a distance; and
- the 'intersubjectivity' of learning at a distance.

The status of the learning achieved

Indications of the status accorded the learning achieved by distance students come from:

- the extent to which other educational institutions recognize the studies for credit transfer purposes;
- the acceptance of the degrees and diplomas awarded as qualifying students to go on to higher level studies;
- the recognition of the awards by employers; and
- the esteem in which the distance teaching institutions and their awards are held in the community at large.

The status of distance programmes can be measured and data collected for evaluation on the extent to which other educational institutions recognize the studies for credit transfer; the acceptance of the distance degrees for higher level studies; and the recognition of the awards by managers in competitive interviews for employment.

The relative cost of the learning achieved

Keegan and Rumble were concerned here with:

- the cost efficiency of distance universities relative to conventional universities or to other modes of internal operation which the distance universities could adopt;
- the cost effectiveness of distance universities relative to conventional universities - the concept of cost effectiveness tries to weigh the relative value of the outputs in qualitative terms;
- the cost benefits of distance and traditional university education, in which the costs of the education provided and the benefits (direct and indirect, financial and social) to the individual and society are taken into account; and
- the opportunity cost of education at a distance.

It has been said that teaching at a distance should cost more than conventional education; things at a distance usually do. However, the history of proprietary correspondence schools had shown the way to mass education by demonstrating how large numbers of students could be enrolled in distance programmes at a low average cost, once the initial capital outlay in the development of learning materials had been undertaken. Studies by Wagner and others showed that similar patterns were achievable by government-sponsored distance teaching universities.

CASE STUDIES

Five institutions are evaluated in accordance with the criteria listed. One institution has been chosen from each of the groupings in the typology of Chapter 8, with the Centre de Vanves of the Centre National d'Enseignement à Distance representing the correspondence schools and colleges of Group 1. The institutions have been chosen from differing national education systems, they have different assessment and ideological frameworks. Three of the institutions work normally in English, one in French, and one in German.

GROUP 1. CENTRE NATIONAL D'ENSEIGNEMENT À DISTANCE (CNED) (NATIONAL CENTRE FOR DISTANCE TEACHING, FRANCE)

Institution

The central adminstration of the CNED is at rue de Bercy, Paris, France. Telephone: from UK 01033140027600 or from

USA 01133140027600. The invasion of France led to the creation of the Centre National d'Enseignement par Correspondance (CNEC) by a government decree of 2 December 1939 to meet the needs of school children dislocated by war. In the mid-1980s the name was changed to its present form, CNED, which might be translated as National Centre for Distance Teaching.

Structure

When the annual enrolment at the CNED in Paris reached 150,000 in the early 1970s a major structural change was achieved. Administrative control of programmes was divided into six centres: Paris, Grenoble, Lille, Lyon, Rouen, and Toulouse. A seventh centre at Rennes was added in 1982.

By a decree of 7 May 1988 the governing body of the CNED (*Conseil d'Administration*) was restructured to comprise representatives of industry, politics, and universities. A protocol of 30 March 1988 on university distance education in France set up a standing committee of the two education ministries, the Director of the CNED and the vice-chancellors of nine French universities.

Staffing

The full-time staff of 1,900 are all employed by the Ministry of Education on the same terms as teachers in French schools. Some of them have been assigned to the CNED because of physical or psychological disabilities and could not be transferred back to the face-to-face system. In addition 1,000 staff are employed for technological and higher education subjects. Many of these staff work full-time from their own homes, thus saving enormously on plant and buildings.

Students and courses

Each year in the late 1980s nearly a quarter of a million students enrol with the CNED from 107 countries (see Table 11.1). Of the 1988 enrolment 15 per cent represents the original mandate of primary and secondary schooling at a distance. Access is provided throughout the world, as it is traditional for French government and business officials, who are on assignment overseas, to enrol their children in the full

French school programme at the CNED for the years in which the family is outside France.

Table 11.1 Annual enrolment at the Centre National d'Enseignement à Distance

Year	Student enrolments
1940	War years
1945	1,413
1950	8,300
1955	30,000
1960	61,000
1965	109,000
1970	146,000
1975	180,000
1980	197,000
1985	225,000
1989	240,000

Source: Renseignements statistiques du CNED.

Adults make up 85 per cent of the students, and are enrolled in every level from post-literacy and numeracy to the equivalent of post-graduate university level courses (see Table 11.2).

Success and quantity of provision

For students in compulsory education aged 6-16 drop-out is not a phenomenon. Students pass easily from classroom education to correspondence and back. Those students resident in France receive a 2-hour visit from a CNED teacher to their house (or hospital etc.) once a week. Students overseas receive comprehensive correspondence tuition from a personal tutor-counsellor assigned to them.

For an analysis of drop-outs at the CNED the researcher can establish from government statistics the number of candidates (*étudiants admissibles*) who studied at the CNED and the number who studied face-to-face. When the results are published the researcher can establish the number and percentage of successful students who studied at a distance and the number and percentage of successful (*étudiants reçus*) students who studied face-to-face.

Table 11.2 Distribution of programmes between the CNED centres at Grenoble, Rennes, Lille, Lyon, Rouen, Toulouse, and Vanves (Paris) in 1988

CNED Centre	*Programmes*	
	Children	*Adults*
Grenoble	Electronics certificates	
	Secondary education	Teacher education
		Sport and Tourism
		Physical education
Lille		Public service education
	Secretarial, accounting certificates	
Lyon		Nursing
		Public service qualifications
		Technical teachers
Rennes		Matriculation
		Biotechnology
		Breton
Rouen	Primary education	CAPES (Teacher education)
Toulouse	Secondary education	Basic education
		Teacher education
Vanves, Paris	Industrial certificates	
	Matriculation	
	Advanced industrial and commercial certificate	
		Adult education
		Modern languages
		Continuing teacher education (in service)
		DEUG (2 year university degree)
		CAPES - CAPET (postgraduate teacher education)
		Agrégation

Source: Renseignements statistiques du CNED.

The CNED annually reports very creditable results in national competitive examinations, with results in humanities subjects being somewhat better than results in sciences and technology.

Quality of provision and status

CNED printed materials are functional. An A4 portrait format with a typeface that gives an average of 22 words per line and over 40 lines per page gives a density of presentation that is relieved only rarely by line drawings. Margins are minimal (average 1.5 cm on both sides) and use of headings, and other layout devices is sparse.

On the other hand the quality of CNED's audio materials is excellent and tapes at all levels and in languages as diverse as Russian and Chinese make up an audio component of extensive quantity and quality.

The status of the qualification is guaranteed by government and employment is guaranteed for the graduates of the distance system if they are successful in winning a place in the quota of successful candidates.

Course development

Course development is by the individual full-time staff member, usually in consultation with colleagues in the same discipline. The materials are edited, commented upon, and approved by the head of department and sent to the production department for development. Extensive use is made of audio materials in music and language courses.

Student support services

The main teaching strategies of the CNED for preparing its students for the national French examinations, once the audio and printed materials have been distributed, is correspondence tuition from a tutor-counsellor, often a full-time staff member, and occasional, voluntary face-to-face sessions.

Costs

The CNED provides full-time staffing for the authorship of

distance teaching materials, for the design and production of the materials and for student support services, with each student being linked to a personal tutor-counsellor at least for the length of one course. Thus most of the CNED budget goes on full-time staff. In 1987 this was FF116,590,000.

Economies are made in contrast to other systems by the availability of full-time teaching staff to work on courses at various levels in the same discipline and from the use of the same production staff for the development of courses in all sectors.

The media mix is conservative with print dominating the learning materials, and correspondence, audio-cassettes, and telephone being the main forms of support. In some parts of the system offices are provided only for senior staff with many full-time staff working full-time from home.

GROUP 2. THE OPEN UNIVERSITY OF THE UNITED KINGDOM (OUUK)

Institution

The Open University is at Walton Hall, Milton Keynes, UK. Telephone: from UK 090874066 or from USA 0114490874066.

Structure

The Open University was created by Royal Charter in 1969 and enrolled its first students in 1971. The executive head is the Vice-Chancellor, assisted by four Pro-Vice-Chancellors. Like other British universities it has a bi-cameral government structure. The Council is the executive governing body and is chaired by the Pro-Chancellor. The Senate, which determines academic policy, is chaired by the Vice-Chancellor.

Staffing

The Open University employs about 2,000 full-time staff in academic or administrative positions at Milton Keynes and at thirteen regional offices throughout Britain. In addition there are British Broadcasting Corporation staff and 4,000 part-time tutors and 2,000 part-time tutor-counsellors. Most of the part-time staff are employed full-time by another tertiary institution.

Students and courses

Since its inception in 1971 the OUUK has given 870,000 UK residents the possibility of applying for enrolment for a university degree at a distance. Over 375,000 have enrolled (see Table 11.3).

Table 11.3 Applications for undergraduate degree programme and initial enrolments at the OUUK from 1971 to 1989

Year	Applications	Cumulative	Initial Registration	Cumulative
1971	40,817		24,220	
1972	34,222	75,039	20,501	44,721
1973	30,414	105,433	16,895	61,616
1974	34,017	139,470	14,976	76,592
1975	49,550	189,020	20,045	96,637
1976	51,450	240,470	17,159	113,796
1977	48,252	288,722	20,097	133,893
1978	42,833	331,555	21,000	154,893
1979	40,235	371,790	21,140	176,033
1980	45,125	419,444	19,448	195,481
1981	42,373	461,817	20,332	214,813
1982	45,667	507,484	25,311	241,124
1983	43,332	550,816	25,613	266,737
1984	41,495	592,311	21,591	288,328
1985	49,691	642,002	19,366	307,694
1986	56,077	698,079	20,147	327,861
1987	56,820	754,899	22,416	350,277
1988	59,336	814,235	25,041	375,318
1989	56,314	870,549		

Source: Open University statistics.

In the late 1980s the annual enrolment was well over 100,000 per year with students studying in (i) the under-graduate programme for the BA (Open), (ii) a post-graduate programme, (ii) the associate student programme, and (iv) a

Table 11.4 Open University BA (Open) graduates by annual cohort with total graduates and total finally registered students 1971–1987

Year	1971	1972	1973	1974	1975	1976	1977	1978	1979	1980	1981	1982	1983	1984	1985	1986	1987	Total Graduates	Total Students
1971	895																	895	19,581
1972	3,314	321																3,635	31,902
1973	2,625	2,300	252															5,177	38,424
1974	1,643	1,744	1,862	218														5,468	42,636
1975	1,249	1,357	1,492	1,698	1													6,025	49,358
1976	543	1,124	1,065	1,251	228	172												5,971	50,994
1977	318	553	876	855	1,811	1,417	5											5,591	55,397
1978	194	284	449	837	1,370	1,101	1,720	8										5,842	58,778
1979	124	209	262	448	1,084	918	1,312	157	16									6,281	60,579
1980	88	145	171	229	575	1,031	1,077	1,618	218	31								6,524	61,007
1981	85	99	127	158	365	536	1,206	1,238	1,735	209	26							8,447	59,968
1982	57	89	98	118	213	328	637	1,041	1,207	1,470	126	27						5,567	63,119
1983	35	61	66	73	159	178	380	1,146	939	957	811	140	34					5,934	60,403
1984	38	50	42	71	129	153	272	644	1,098	852	1,052	836	139	26				6,678	66,763
1985	32	36	30	47	83	120	153	399	722	1,136	1,275	1,613	827	142	32			6,602	67,433
1986	23	37	39	35	64	80	121	262	372	656	733	1,255	1,364	762	117	38		6,564	66,191
1987							194	163	259	360	1,387	1,571	1,152	1,192	508	86	41		71,567
Total	11,263	8,409	6,851	6,038	7,203	6,035	7,077	6,676	6,566	5,671	5,410	5,442	3,516	2,122	657	124	41	89,101	
Graduates as a % of new students	57.52	53.51	54.03	53.26	48.57	49.34	46.73	2.73	44.20	40.44	37.54	30.62	19.95	13.74	4.74	0.86	0.23		
	19,581	15,716	12,680	11,336	14,830	12,231	15,246	5,622	14,854	14,022	14,410	17,772	17,627	15,446	13,870	14,482	16,043		

Source: Open University statistics.

wide range of further education programmes at a distance, from mother and child courses to the Open Business School for managers.

In 1987 45.6 per cent of undergraduates were female, the median age was 32 and only 25 per cent of students were under 22. Teachers had dropped from 40 per cent of enrolled students in 1971 to 13.8 per cent, with housewives totalling 17.7 per cent.

The percentage of new undergraduate students who were unqualified for study at other British universities (less than two 'A' levels) had risen from 27 per cent in 1971 to 42.3 per cent in 1987.

Success and quantity of provision

The OUUK has largely solved the drop-out problem that has been a feature of many other distance education systems for adults (see Table 11.4). Table 11.4 shows that nearly 90,000 students have graduated with the BA (Open) degree. The sceptics who claimed at the foundation of the OUUK that no more than 10 per cent of any intake would eventually graduate have been resoundingly answered. OU statistics show that about 50 per cent of every cohort will always graduate, unless there is an abrupt change of statistical pattern. Up to 45 per cent of each year's undergraduate cohort is graduating in a highly acceptable 6 years.

Quality of provision and status

The OUUK broke new ground in distance education by the quality, complexity, and comprehensiveness of its learning materials, both print and non-print. The A4 profile layout with the OU logo became an easily recognized standard, not only for the OU's students, but in bookshops throughout the UK, and on the reading lists of many conventional universities. The materials were characterized by careful structuring and sequencing of content together with sophisticated layout and design.

The clear design of the OUUK system is to provide education at a distance and not just information giving (Keegan 1981). Evidences of this are:

• the continuity of concern for students studying at a distance (Sewart 1978);

- the structuring of the system for the avoidance of avoidable drop-out;
- the identification of students who are at risk;
- the wide range of student support services including compulsory residential schools; and
- provision of a personal tutor-counsellor and a variety of optional or compulsory contact activities.

The OUUK quickly shed its correspondence image and sought to insert itself within its first decade into the fabric of British educational and political life.

Course development

Courses are written by course teams. A first-year course can have as many as twenty full-time OU or BBC staff assigned to it plus consultants. The course team designs a total learning package comprising printed materials, home experiment kits, BBC television programmes, audio and video cassettes, teaching strategies, and induction and training programmes for those who will tutor and counsel students enrolled in the course 3-10 years later.

Following early discussions on content and teaching strategies, responsibility for various parts or blocks of the course, and for scriptwriting and kit composition is assigned to course authors. Several drafts of most materials are often produced, the later ones incorporating suggestions and criticisms made at meetings of the course team.

Student support services

The OUUK developed a particularly rich structure of student support services which was in many ways the central innovation of the system (Keegan 1979). The system, providing linking between materials and learning, included at least nine interlocking components, many of which were optional to the student. These structures came under the control of the OUUK's Regional Tutorial Services Department and were described by Sewart (1978) as a 'continuity of concern for the student studying at a distance':

- the tutor-counsellor who follows the student throughout his/her university career;
- the tutor available for consultation on an individual course;

- thirteen regional offices providing a decentralized focus for the administration of tuition, counselling, and student support systems;
- a study centre within easy travelling distance where the student can meet other students and use facilities;
- tutorials at regular intervals;
- computerized student records that can pick up problems in students' progress and anticipate drop-out;
- Kosmat analysis – a computerized weighting of the grades given by tutors on all assignments against the national average;
- residential summer schools; and
- a student association with regional branches.

Costs

The cost structures of the OUUK are now well known and have been referred to extensively in Chapter 10. It still spends large amounts of monies on broadcast television and this has been criticized on economic grounds and queried by Bates (1981) in terms of educational effectiveness. It also spends large amounts of money on regional and student support services and this has been queried also. Defenders of this expenditure (Sewart 1978) claim that this is the only way to keep students in the system and to provide university education rather than instruction.

GROUP 3. THE DEPARTMENT OF INDEPENDENT STUDY OF THE UNIVERSITY OF FLORIDA AT GAINESVILLE

Institution

The Department of Independent Study by Correspondence, University of Florida, Gainesville, Florida 32611, USA. Telephone: from UK 01019043921711, from USA 9043921711.

Structure

The University of Florida is one of the nine public universities which comprise Florida's state university system.

One of the many administrative structures within the University of Florida is the Division of Continuing Education. The purpose of the Division of Continuing Education is to contribute to a learning society by helping students pursue educational interests at home, on campus and in the community, while they are actively working or meeting personal and family obligations.

The Department of Independent Study by Correspondence is one of the departments of the Division of Continuing Education. This department has been designated in state law as the only distance education programme to serve all the public universities in the Florida system.

Staffing

The director of the Department of Independent Study has a staff of 20 full-time administrators who run a single centralized office through which all registrations and assignments flow. In 1988 the Department utilized 140 faculty who were employed in the academic departments of several of Florida's public universities; no faculty members are employed full-time in distance education.

The Vice-President for Academic Affairs of the university supervises all academic areas, and the deans of the respective colleges under him supervise the conventional staff. The Dean of Continuing Education reports to the Vice-President for Academic Affairs, and so in an organizational sense continuing education is parallel to but separately organized from the faculties in the colleges of the university.

Conventional staff are utilized as part-time employees of the Division of Continuing Education for all university credit courses at a distance and on campus, teaching in an overload status for which they draw additional compensation. High school teachers from the university's Laboratory School, also on the regular faculty, teach most of the high school courses offered at a distance by the university.

Students and courses

The total enrollment in the department in 1987-88 was 8,616. Of these 51 per cent were in undergraduate university courses, 16 per cent in high school programmes and 33 per cent in non-credit courses. With 8,618 enrolments the University of Florida was one of the largest of the 70 United States universities affiliated to the Independent Study Division of the National University Continuing Education Association (NUCEA).

Typical student groups were: full-time students who, due to courses being unavailable on-campus or job conflicts, take external courses as an alternative; adults working on external degrees elsewhere; and high school students who must make up missed or failed courses. There are limitations imposed by most of the faculties of United States universities on the use of independent study credits towards degree programmes and in many cases one is not permitted to complete a full degree at a distance. This is particularly so at Master's level.

Success and quantity of provision

There is a less than 2 per cent failure in courses done by independent study, though some who are doing poor work may elect not to complete their courses and thus avoid a failing grade. In 1987-88 there were 8,618 registrations and 3,890 completions; 274 students formally dropped their enrolments, usually receiving a partial refund of fees paid. Another 1,197 students extended their expiring enrolment through the payment of an additional fee.

Since 45 per cent of the students completed their courses, there was a 55 per cent non-completion rate for the year. There is not adequate data to distinguish those who have permanently dropped out from those who have temporarily discontinued their studies.

Quality of provision and status

Each university course study guide is prepared by a regular member of the faculty, basing the content on the course he teaches for his academic department on the campus.

Once the course study guide has been edited, illustrated and published, the content is co-ordinated with and approved by the academic department chairman before the course is opened to student enrolment. Students are required to obtain a counsellor's permission to enrol if they plan to apply the credit earned to meet degree requirements. Thus, to the extent possible, the independent study programme is integrated with the conventional system.

The university courses fall under the accreditation system of the Southern Association of Colleges and Schools, one of the regional accrediting associations that accredit all university education in the United States. Individual courses that may be applied to degrees are offered, but not an external degree.

Evaluation

Non-credit courses do not require accreditation, but each is co-ordinated and approved by the state agency or professional association that establishes continuing professional education requirements in its field.

Course development

Each course is prepared by the faculty member who is to teach it. Course production staff provide support in the form of editing, word processing, obtaining needed copyright permission and artwork, and desktop publishing. Most courses are limited to illustrations and diagrams printed in the study guides. Also used are audio tapes (both commercial and locally prepared), video tapes (prepared by the university's College of Engineering), cloth samples, rock kits, seed kits and sets of 35mm slides.

In all courses the course evaluation standards of the National University Continuing Education Association are rigorously applied. This has resulted in national awards for course excellence.

Student support services

Student support services include toll-free phone lines serving students anywhere in the US; an extension library that provides books, periodicals, and photocopies of articles without charge upon request (postage is paid by the library both ways); and limited advice and referral. Numerous instructors regularly meet in their offices with independent study students on an appointment basis.

Costs

The total cost per year (1988) of the distance education system was $1,313,122. This included salaries, expenses, instructor grading and other part-time services. The sources of funds for the 1987–88 academic year were: state government 32 per cent, non-credit course fees 38 per cent, book store operations 23 per cent, and reserves 7 per cent.

The non-credit course fees combine high school and non-credit fees paid by students; these programmes are required to be self-supporting. The book store is also required to be self-supporting. Income from state government is intended to offset the cost of operating the university credit programme. Fees collected from students for registration in university courses are returned to the state government; these amounted to $319,616 in 1987-88.

GROUP 4. DIE FERNSTUDIUMABTEILUNG DER KARL-MARX UNIVERSITAT LEIPZIG (DISTANCE EDUCATION DEPARTMENT OF THE UNIVERSITY OF LEIPZIG)

Institution

The University of Leipzig in the German Democratic Republic was founded in 1409. The address of the Distance Education Department is Ritterstrasse 14, Leipzig 7010, GDR. Telephone: from UK 01037417190 or from USA 01137417190.

Structure

The university has a Directorate for Further Education which has two sections, the Distance Education Department and a further and evening study department. The Director of the Distance Education Department has two responsibilities - he reports to the Vice-Chancellor (*Rektor*) of the University of Leipzig and to the Central Institute for University Distance Education of the Ministry of Higher and Further Education which is in the city of Dresden.

The Department of Distance Education has a consultation centre at the university and an office for distance education within each faculty which teaches at a distance (six of the twenty-nine faculties at the University of Leipzig).

Staffing

Conventional full-time staff is involved in face-to-face education (*Direktstudium*) and in distance education and evening courses (*Fernstudium* and *Abendstudium*). Part-time staff are not employed.

Students and courses

In 1988 enrolment at the University of Leipzig was 15,000, of whom 2,000 were distance students. Most of the distance

students were studying for the full degree (*Diplom*) programme which takes 5½ years at a distance. The remaining
distance students were doing more advanced post-graduate
degrees.

The average age of distance students is 28 years. All are in
full-time employment and are sponsored by their companies
for enrolment in the distance degree programmes.

Why do they not study face-to-face? The first reason is
financial: government subsidies for conventional students are
low (200 Marks per month). One can earn five times that
amount in one's company and study at a distance. Second,
workers are needed to contribute to the GDP as the GDR has
a labour shortage. Promotion within the company is practically
guaranteed on the completion of the distance degree. Finally,
distance students receive by law one day's paid study leave per
week (48 days per year).

Success and quantity of provision

Twenty of the fifty-four universities and institutions of higher
education in the GDR teach at a distance. Of the 130,000
university students in the year 1988, 14,000 were studying by
distance education.

Drop-outs occur especially at the beginning of the distance
university courses, but 70 per cent of students complete the
Diplom within the allocated time of 5½ years.

Quality of provision and status

The University of Leipzig accredits the distance degrees as it
does the direct ones. The special printed materials that are the
basis of distance study are used both by distance and conventional students.

It is estimated (Möhle 1988:3) that there were 1.7 million
university graduates in the GDR in 1988 and that no less than
one-quarter of these obtained their degrees at a distance. In
many practical disciplines, like horticulture, a distance award
is often preferred as the integration of theory and practice is
ensured by this method of study.

The goal is education in the wider sense rather than a
narrow training; the development of creative personalities is
a specific aim of distance provision.

Course development

Course development takes place at the Central Office of Distance Education at Dresden. The Ministry selects leading professors in the discipline from around the GDR and brings them to Dresden where there is a permanent group of production staff.

The University of Leipzig is usually represented in the course development in those faculties in which it teaches at a distance: Statistics and Economics; Marxism-Leninism; Theory of Culture; Journalism.

Student support services

A distance enrolment is a three-way arrangement between the student, the company, and the university so that support comes both from the university and the company. In return, the thesis in the last year of the degree is usually written on an aspect of company research.

The basic structure is the consultation at the University of Leipzig's Consultation Centre. Once a fortnight for a whole day the distance students attend the consultations or seminars in the five or six subjects in which they are enrolled.

This is made possible by subsidized travel and by the fact that they have one day per week paid study leave from work.

Costs

Distance education is an integral part of the GDR higher university system. As Leipzig is one of the twenty universities designated to provide distance courses in a variety of disciplines for the whole country, the total budget comes from the Ministry of Higher Education. The fees for students are small (10 Marks per month) and are usually paid by the student's company.

GROUP 5. THE DEPARTMENT OF EXTERNAL STUDIES OF THE UNIVERSITY OF NEW ENGLAND

Institution

The University of New England is at Armidale, New South Wales, Australia 2351. Telephone: from UK 0106167733333 or

Evaluation

from USA 0116167733333.

Structure

The University of New England's Vice-Chancellor is the chief executive and reports to the University Council chaired by the Chancellor. There are, in 1988, two Pro-Vice-Chancellors, one for full-time students and one for part-time students. The Department of External Studies comes within the purview of the Pro-Vice-Chancellor for part-time students.

Staffing

The Department of External Studies has a full-time administrative staff of forty, headed by the Director of External Studies. The University of New England has 370 full-time academic staff who are involved in distance education. Part-time staff are not usually employed.

Students and courses

The enrolment of the university in 1988 was 9,100: 5,900 studying externally, the remaining 3,200 internal.

When the university was inaugurated in 1955 it taught both internally and externally. The external provision was originally to meet the needs of a shortage of graduate teachers in New South Wales. In 1964 82 per cent of the external enrolments were teachers and numbered 2,263; by 1983 the proportion of teachers had fallen to 28 per cent.

Today the University of New England gives external access to bachelor degrees, post-graduate diplomas, and masters degrees for twenty-seven separate awards in a wide range of disciplines.

Of the external students 70 per cent are studying for undergraduate degrees; the remaining 30 per cent for post-graduate qualifications.

The student population is heterogeneous. In 1988 53 per cent were female, ages were from 20 to 80 and students had varied educational and work backgrounds. Students enrol externally because of isolation from tertiary institutions, because of family commitments, work commitments, or a preference for individual study.

Success and quantity of provision

In any one year 82-85 per cent of distance students who submit for final assessment are successful. In terms of university merit lists and awards external students figure prominently.

Drop-out is highest among new students. Since 1983 there has been a noticeable downward trend in withdrawal rates from 26.9 per cent in 1983 to 16.3 per cent in 1987. As there is no time limit on first degree completion, students 'drop-in' and 'drop-out' of the external system as their circumstances dictate.

Quality of provision and status

The status of learning at a distance and of awards is accepted as being of the same standard as the conventional part of the university. The degrees and awards are the same for distance students as for the on-campus students and are accredited by the university.

The external courses provide a university education; there is a minor element of training in a limited number of programmes. The quality of the external programme is underpinned by the following provisions:

- compulsory residential summer schools for each unit;
- the obligation on distance students to see their university and enjoy a brief period of traditional university life as a full-time student in residence;
- optional weekend seminars;
- visits by full-time faculty to student groups or to individual students on farms; and
- distance students being brought into contact with the best brains of the university, not part-time staff.

Course development

Courses are usually designed by individual academics supported by specialist development staff.

Print is the medium used in most courses and is supported by audio (large proportion of courses), audio-vision (fairly common), and video (small proportion). The use of interactive radio and TV is increasing in the late 1980s.

Student support services

Heavy reliance is placed on the telephone, mail and the fax. Residential schools are compulsory in approximately 70 per cent of all external courses. These are held mainly in Armidale in the New South Wales country about 300 km north-west of Sydney. Voluntary weekend schools are conducted in Sydney and other centres in New South Wales.

Student support services are centralized through the Department of External Studies and individual on-campus academics. Support is also provided in a decentralized way through graduate representatives, regional advisers, and a Sydney External Studies Centre.

Costs

The total cost of the distance system was $16,000,000 (Australia) in 1988. The source of funds was almost entirely from the recurrent grant of the Federal Australian Government.

REFERENCES

Bates, A.W. (1981) 'Towards a better framework for evaluating the effectiveness of educational media', *British Journal of Educational Technology*, 12, 215-33.

Keegan, D. (1979) 'The Regional Tutorial Services of the Open University: a case study', *ZIFF Papiere 29*, Hagen: Fernuniversität.

Keegan, D. (1981) 'Drop-outs at the Open University', *Australian Journal of Education* 24, (1), 44-55.

Keegan, D. and Rumble, G. (1982) 'The DTUs: an appraisal', in G. Rumble and K. Harry (eds) *The Distance Teaching Universities*, London: Croom Helm, pp. 222-50.

Möhle, H. (1988) *Social Development of the GDR - Consequences for Higher-Level Distance Education*, Leipzig: Karl-Marx University.

Sewart, D. (1978) 'Continuity of concern for students studying at a distance', *ZIFF Papiere 18*, Hagen: Fernuniversität.

Chapter Twelve

CONCLUSION

> That's what I'm trying to do. Sing a better song.
> *Educating Rita*, 1983

Distance education is a little-studied area of education which is growing in importance annually. As a more industrialized form of educational provision it is well adapted to the developments of new communications technologies and brings to education many of the strengths and dangers of industrialization. It is also adapted to the growth of privacy in post-industrial societies which focuses many of the functions of living on the individual's residence with a concomitant loss of the sense of community in society.

The conclusions from the study are many and varied but are not put forward here as judgements which are to be considered normative for practice. Rather they are put forward as suggestions for research by scholars and invitations to others to contribute to our knowledge of the theory and practice of distance education.

Among the most important are:

- distance education is a coherent and distinct field of educational endeavour;
- distance education is a distinct field of education, parallel to and a complement of conventional education. It has its own didactic laws, administrative procedures, and characteristic buildings and plant;
- distance education is a needed component of many national education systems;
- the correct term for this sector of education is 'distance education';
- it is possible to propose a coherent definition of distance education which distinguishes it from other areas of educational activity;

- distance education institutions can be classified into five major groupings;
- distance systems can be cheaper but this depends on a complex range of factors, some of which may affect the quality of provision;
- distance systems have inherent difficulties with the quantity, quality, and status of provision;
- cohesive and competently administered systems can solve the problems of quantity, quality, and status of provision (examples are given of institutions which appear to have achieved acceptable solutions); and
- distance education is a legitimate field of academic enquiry.

The study accepts Pagney's (1980) position that distance education is complementary to conventional provision. Distance education is the normal provision of education for the working man and woman, for the taxpayer, the home-maker, those who do not wish to attend a conventional institution, and sometimes for their children. Conventional education is the normal provision for others.

No government can provide schools, colleges, and universities near the workplace of every citizen and few can provide for citizens outside the 5–25 years age bracket. Distance education is a needed component of most national education systems.

As the 1980s progressed towards the 1990s the loss of community involvement in many western societies and the consequent growth of privatization of living was seen by some as further indications of the permanency of education at a distance (Smith 1987).

The challenge taken up by distance educators is to provide at a distance an educational experience that achieves parity with conventional provision in quality, quantity, and status.

CURRENT ISSUES

The rationale for distance education does not lie in the notion that there is something wrong with conventional education that distance education should correct. This is a dangerous cul-de-sac. The reply can be withering:

A few years ago 'non-traditional learning' was touted as a mechanism to democratise education. Today ministers of education are happily hacking at 'traditional' institutions which are easily replaced by 'distance education'. There is a vast irony in all this because distance education was supposed to help democratise educational processes; few anticipated it would be a weapon used to beat the heads of institutions where learners and teachers have the temerity to gather together to learn in groups.

(Boshier 1985:139)

Since the publication of the first edition of this book there has been some discussion of a convergence between distance and conventional education or of a blurring of the distinctions between them. Smith and Kelly (1987) take one side in this discussion; Dieuzeide (1985) the other.

Smith and Kelly (1987) write that the methods of teaching in distance education and mainstream on-campus education at post-compulsory level are beginning to converge. Traditional teaching methods, they state, are in some instances being abandoned or modified in favour of a resource-based approach which de-emphasizes the teacher as the main source of knowledge.

Dieuzeide (1985) shows that distance education has progressed from commercial provision to public and political involvement in the last 40 years. He sees distance education as a technical commodity of interest to innovators and political realists who want the cheapest provision for the national economy. Dieuzeide hesitates to give distance education the role of an educational panacea because it runs counter, he claims, to the face-to-face nature of the educational process which, in most cultures, is based on face-to-face contact and oral communication (*fondée sur le contact et l'oralité*). If the student is placed at home and studies primarily from materials and is not invited to attend the university in which he or she is enrolled then all the cultural imperatives cited by Dieuzeide come into play.

There seems to be little likelihood, therefore, that the administrators of conventional programmes will want to merge with programmes in which children and adults study away from educational institutions and outside the oral, group-based structures of western culture, even if an attempt is made to recreate such structures electronically.

NON-TRADITIONAL OR CONVENTIONAL?

In *The Distance Teaching Universities* Rumble and I tried to trace an evolution from the provision of university courses at the residential universities of the 1800s, to the introduction of non-residential full-time programmes late in the last century, to the introduction of part-time night-time courses in this century and the creation of the distance universities in the 1970s. If there is any validity in this pattern and if one accepts that the first three stages are today seen as conventional provision, the question remains: can a distance university become conventional? The beginnings of an answer are provided by Perry:

> Academics all over Britain accept that the Open University has succeeded, that distance learning works and that the Open University graduates are as good as any others. They (these graduates) have been accepted by every other British University in postgraduate courses without question. The quality of the courses is seen and is commended by the academics in other universities. But emotionally, many of them don't accept it at all. Emotionally there still is a strong feeling that on-campus teaching in the face-to-face situation is the one way of actually teaching and that this is the vital thing in order to train scholars for the future. It may take decades rather than years to overcome this emotional reaction. (Perry 1986:15)

Parity of esteem can be achieved by developing a satisfactory theoretical structure for distance education supported by an informed analysis of good distance education practice.

STUDY OF THE FOUNDATIONS OF DISTANCE EDUCATION

Study of this field is hampered because the two major studies are not available to those who read only English. Peters' *Die didaktische Struktur des Fernunterrichts. Untersuchungen zu einer industrialisierten Form des Lehrens und Lehrnens* has never been translated and there is little likelihood that Henri and Kaye's recent *Le Savoir à Domicile. Pédagogie et problematique de la formation à distance* will appear in English. Both books contain valuable contributions to the theory of distance education.

This book has sought to give a first overview of the field and highlight areas for further research. The 100 years' history of the field makes research difficult, as does its breadth. Dieuzeide (1985:33) working from UNESCO statistics in the mid-1980s estimates that the number of students studying in the world at six hundred million, with ten million studying at a distance. Of the distance students he claims that one-third are in Russia or China. Dieuzeide's data look reasonably valid but such statistics may prove daunting rather than encouraging to the researcher.

The chequered history of the use of mechanical and electronic media in distance education, and the resurgence in the mid-1980s of well-researched studies of distance education for children (Vivian 1986) clearly distinguish the work of the distance education researcher from the two nearest fields within educational research: educational technology and adult education.

Although there are some similarities between these fields the distance theorist must, nevertheless, develop positions which are equally valid for children and for adults, and which treat technology in education as a substitute for, rather than as a supplement to, the interpersonal communication of mainstream education.

REFERENCES

Boshier, R. (1985) Book review. *The International Review of Education* 31(1), 139-40.

Dieuzeide, H. (1985) 'Les enjeux politiques', in F. Henri and A. Kaye (eds) *Le Savoir à Domicile*, Quebec: Téléuniversité.

Henri, F. and Kaye, A. (1985) *Le Savoir à Domicile*, Quebec: Téléuniversité.

Keegan, D. and Rumble, G. (1982) 'Distance teaching at university level', in G. Rumble and K. Harry (eds) *The Distance Teaching Universities*, London: Croom Helm.

Pagney, B. (1980) 'Quels advantages l'enseignement a distance peut-il offrir a l'enseignement formel?', Paper to *EHSC Conference*, April 1980.

Perry, W. (1986) 'Distance education, trends worldwide', in G. van Enckevort *et al.* (eds) *Distance Education and the Adult Learner*, Heerlen: Open Universiteit, pp. 15-20.

Peters, O. (1973) *Die Didaktische Struktur des Fernunterrichts*, Weinheim: Beltz.

Smith, P. (1987) 'Distance education and educational change', in P. Smith and M. Kelly (eds) *Distance Education and the Mainstream*, London: Croom Helm.

Smith, P. and Kelly, M. (1987) (eds) *Distance Education and the Mainstream*, London: Croom Helm.

Vivian, V. (1986) 'Electronic mail in a childrens' distance course: trial and evaluation', *Distance Education* 7(2), 214-36.

ABBREVIATIONS

The following abbreviations are used from time to time especially in lists of references:

CMA	Computer marked assignment
CU	Conventional university
DIFF	Deutsches Institut für Fernstudien, Tübingen
DTU	Distance teaching university
FeU	Fernuniversität-Gesamthochschule, Hagen
ICDE	International Council for Distance Education
OU	Open University
OUUK	Open University of the United Kingdom
TMA	Tutor marked assignment
UNE	University of New England, Armidale, Australia
UNED	Universidad Nacional de Educación a Distancia
UNISA	University of South Africa, Pretoria
ZIFF	Zentrales Institut für Fernstudienforschung, Fernuniversität, Hagen.

INDEX

access, 172, 186, 191, 202
adult education, 7, 9, 126, 208
adult learners, 8
agrégation, 188
Alberta Correspondence School, 126, 144
Ascent of Man, The, 23
assignments, 112, 126, 195
Association of European Correspondence Schools, 150
Athabasca University, 145, 170, 175
audio-cassettes, 41, 127, 133, 138, 189
audio-conferencing, 41
audio-visual aids, 22
autonomy 43, 57, 62, 65, 69, 89, 124, 127, 137, 143, 174

Berlin School of Didactics, 75, 81
British Broadcasting Corporation, 154, 190
broadcast radio, 118, 164
broadcast television, 11, 39, 40, 118, 139, 164, 168

Carnegie Committee 20
Centre National d'Enseig-
nement à Distance (CNED), 34, 123, 125, 130, 144, 162, 185-7
Centre de Télé-enseignement universitaire, 132
choice of media, 151, 172, 174
Civilisation 23
closed circuit television 61
communications technology, 4, 35, 40, 105, 130, 151, 171, 203
computer-aided learning, 23
computer conferencing, 41, 76, 116, 152
computer-marked assignments (CMAs), 24, 43, 86
consultation model, 132-4, 146, 154
continuing education, 100
control theory, 14-16
conventional education, 3, 5, 20
convergence, 207
correspondence education 29, 30, 33, 51, 60, 73, 85, 91, 126
correspondence schools, 11, 12, 42, 74, 80, 121, 125-6, 127, 129, 130, 144, 155, 162, 164, 185
correspondence study, 18,